The House of Dracula

A comedy-horror

Martin Downing

Samuel French - London
New York - Toronto - Hollywood

THE HOUSE OF DRACULA

Originally performed by The Screaming Blue Murder Theatre Company at the Civic Theatre, Leeds—Hallowe'en 1991—with the following cast:

Baron von Frankenstein	Gilbert Robinson
Baroness von Frankenstein	Stephanie Wright
Ygor	Keith Baxter
Frau Lurker	Jo McCarey
Harry Talbot	Anthony Bentley
Isabel Channing	Lisa Lowe
Count Dracula	Simon Wellings
Countess Dracula	Pam Jones
Doctor Jekyll	Orazio Rea
Groat	Simon Motin
Ethel	Michelle Greenley
Ka-Seet	Matthew Brighton
Spectre	Chaz Elliott
Creature	Tim Stephenson

The play was directed by **Jo McCarey**

The action of the play takes place in a grim castle near Borgo Pass, Transylvania.

ACT I Late evening, Walpurgisnacht

ACT II Scene 1 Half an hour later
   Scene 2 Immediately following
   Scene 3 Shortly afterwards

Technical personnel for the original production

Stage Manager	Michelle Hainsworth
A.S.M.	Debbie Burton
Lighting	Peter Waddicor
Sound	Julian Deering
Crew	Steven Crabb
	Stephen Earle
Settings and Props	Keith Baxter
	Orazio Rea
Specialist Make-up	Steve Hadi
Costumes	Micheal Downing
F.O.H. Manager	Eric Tillotson

CHARACTERS

Baron Victor von Frankenstein, a scientist
Baroness Elisabeth von Frankenstein, his wife
Ygor, his butler
Frau Lurker, his housekeeper
Harry Talbot, a werewolf
Isabel Channing, a bitch
Count Vlad Dracula, the King of Vampires
Countess Ilona Dracula, his Queen
Doctor Henry Jekyll, a schizophrenic
Groat, a zombie
Ethel, a vampire
Ka-Seet, a mummy
A Spectre
A Creature

AUTHOR'S NOTE

In any programme, so as not to give too much away, it is better to list **Jekyll** as **The Doctor**.

The **Spectre** and the **Creature** are intended to be played by the same actor and, if you are stuck for men, **Groat** can double **Ka-Seet**. If this is the case all **Groat**'s business in Act II and his one line should be given to **Ethel**, apart from his bits in the chase sequence, which can be covered by the **Spectre**.

The tune for Frau Lurker's sung entrance in ACT II Scene 1 comes from *The Pirates of Penzance* by Messrs Gilbert and Sullivan. Similarly, if the actress wishes to sing the lines "When the night wind howls . . . *etc.*" (ACT II Scene 3), these are derived from *Ruddigore*.

It is important to remember that the play is a comedy-*horror*, and in staging it the sinister elements should be emphasized as much as the humour.

Costume and special effects suggestions follow at the end of the script.

To Mum and Dad, for thirty-four years of love,
loyalty and encouragement.

And to Jo, Keith and all the members
of their company for showing such
faith, friendship and expertise when
staging the first performances of
this play.

CHARACTER DESCRIPTIONS

The Baron: he is 36 years old, of clean-cut appearance and has a forceful, if disillusioned personality.

The Baroness: she is 28, very attractive, but vain, diffident and outspoken.

Ygor: he is of indeterminate age, ugly, scruffy and shambles everywhere. Extrovert and eccentric.

Frau Lurker: she is in her mid-sixties and has a grim, menacing manner. She speaks tersely with a German accent and marches rather than walks.

Talbot: he is a good-looking, athletic but rather irritable American in his early thirties.

Isabel: she is an American in her early twenties, attractive but extremely brash and provocative.

The Count: he appears to be in his mid-forties and speaks with a Romanian accent. His appearance is suave yet sinister and he has great presence.

The Countess: she appears to be in her late thirties, very attractive but rather melancholy. She speaks with a mid-European accent.

Dr Jekyll: he is an outspoken, temperamental Scotsman in his early fifties. A total extrovert. As **Hyde** he is horribly sinister and has to be able to speak and sing with a cockney accent.

Groat: he can be any age. The main thing is he is decayed, uncoordinated and stupid.

Ethel: a pretty bride of Dracula, aged 30. She looks fearsome, but when she speaks she has a warm cockney personality.

Ka-Seet: he should appear to be just like The Mummy from the old films; withered, with only one good arm and leg.

The Spectre: any permutations are possible, i.e. a shrouded ghoul, walled-up monk, drowned warrior.

The Creature: try to follow the suggestion at the end of Act II, but if you can't please avoid the Phantom of the Opera and Frankenstein's monster, both of whom appear in *The House of Frankenstein!*

ACT I

The hall of an ancient castle. Late evening

High stone walls form the framework, and set into these up R is a single arched and mullioned window which overlooks a gloomy courtyard. A heavy arched door opens in from this R and other arched doorways give access to dark passages up R and L. A stone staircase with balustrade leads to the bedrooms up L

Three ornate high-backed chairs stand beneath the window, down R and down L respectively. Between the window and the doorway up R is a carved oak table surmounted by a silver candelabra. A larger table stands beneath the staircase. On top are a number of old-fashioned decanters and glasses

Left of C is a very old sofa with a table at one end. An equally old armchair and table are placed right of C. Up C, standing against the wall, is a large mummy case with a hinged or removable lid. It is colourfully painted with authentic Egyptian hieroglyphics, but at present it is draped with a dark velvet cloth. On either side stand large candleholders

The floor of the hall is paved with stone and, like much of the furniture, it is very dusty. Large cobwebs fill most corners and the walls are ornamented with grim coats of arms, fearsome weaponry and tattered heraldic banners

As the CURTAIN rises a terrific gale is blowing outside the castle and the lights flicker, creating menacing moving shadows throughout the hall

A mysterious veiled woman—the Countess Dracula—stands C reading aloud from a bound volume of poetry amid the gale's intensity

Countess   Once upon a midnight dreary, while I pondered, weak and weary,
Over many a quaint and curious volume of forgotten lore—
While I nodded, nearly napping, suddenly there came a tapping,

There is a brief pounding on the door R

As of someone gently rapping, rapping at the castle door.

A furious pounding this time

'Tis some visitors a-calling at my doorstep— but what for?

Another mad pounding on the door

Baron (*off*) For pity's sake—let us in!
Baroness (*off*) We're being blown to pieces out here!
Countess (*moving to the window*) What a nuisance. What a *bore*.
Baroness (*off; screaming above the gale*) Oh Victor!
Baron (*off; frantically*) Elisabeth! *Come back.*
Baroness (*off; terrified*) I can't. The gale's caught my skirts!
Countess (*peering out of the window; amused*) Up, up—and away!
Baron (*off; shouting*) Grab that creeper! The one by the chimney.
Countess I shouldn't—it's loose.

The Baroness screams off

Baron (*off*) What's wrong?
Baroness (*off*) It's come away from the wall!
Countess (*shaking her head*) I told you.
Baron (*off*) Hold tight! I've got the other end.
Baroness (*off*) Then haul me down!
Baron (*off*) I'm trying—I'm trying. (*Shouting*) What's it like up there?
Baroness (*off*) Dreadful! I feel like a kite.
Countess You look more like Mary Poppins.
Baroness (*off*) Hurry up, will you?
Baron (*off*) Just a few more feet, dearest. Can you see the sea?
Baroness (*off*) No!

The gale starts to fade

Oh look—the wind's dropping.
Countess So are you.

A short scream, a crash and a groan are heard off. The Countess moves towards the doorway L

Baroness (*off; relieved*) Thank goodness for that.
Baron (*off; pained*) You didn't have to land on top of me.
Baroness (*off; brusquely*) Of course I did. Stop moaning!

Reaching the doorway, the Countess turns and waves her hand at the door R, *then exits*

The door opens mysteriously and the Baroness sails in, her hair dishevelled, and clutching a wicker cat-box. She is closely followed by the Baron, who is equally ruffled

Baron (*dusting himself down irritably*) Next time I'll side-step.
Baroness (*putting the cat-box on the sofa*) It won't make an ounce of difference. I've got perfect aim.

She starts adjusting her hair and he scowls. The door R *begins to close and they both stare at it, startled*

(*Gesturing, wide-eyed, as it shuts*) Did you see that?
Baron (*moving to examine it*) An automatic door. Fascinating.
Baroness It's *uncanny.*

Baron (*turning*) You've been to Tesco's?

Baroness Yes—but this is a castle.

Baron Quite. (*Producing a notebook and pen*) And with all those carefully constructed cobwebs—(*glancing up*)—candelabra creating cunning chiaroscuro effects—(*gesturing to the floor*)—and a carpet of centuries-old dust, it's everything one might expect. (*He starts to move round the hall, making notes*)

Baroness (*shuddering*) From a *tip*—yes.

Baron Why can't you think positively, dearest?

Baroness Very well, it's a *positive* tip. (*Running her fingers over the sofa, raising dust*) Look!

Baron Well at least nothing grisly has come to greet us.

Baroness No, we left that to stable the carriage and horses. What was it?

Baron A cross between an orang-utan and Siamese twins. (*Musing*) Someone has clearly taken the maxim "two heads are better than one" to heart.

Baroness (*shuddering*) It was *hideous*.

Baron (*brightly*) But it did give us a lift. Would you have preferred to walk? Think of all those perilous ravines.

Baroness I'm unlikely to forget them, darling. With two wheels constantly teetering over the edge I had a bird's-eye view.

Baron *I* could do with a Birds Eye snack.

Baroness (*angrily*) Oh, how can you be so glib? We almost perished!

Baron Don't be silly. We were in perfectly safe hands.

Baroness And all four of them *hairy*. (*Sitting on the sofa*) I've never been so terrified in my life.

Baron You have—and often. Castle Frankenstein was hardly Shangri-La.

Baroness (*irritably*) Don't remind me.

Baron (*snapping his notebook shut and putting it away*) So control yourself.

There is an eerie noise off and they both jump

(*Bravely*) This outing's nothing untoward. In fact so far it's been exhilarating. We've ridden the Boot Hill Express—cameoed in *Gone with the Wind*——

Baroness (*unfastening the cat-box*) Yes, but abseiling and shooting the rapids on the penultimate leg was *far* from amusing. (*She produces a leafy green "thing" from the box and cradles it*) All that jarring and jolting nearly cost Cabbage his teeth.

Baron You know I can always dig him up a new set.

Baroness Thanks, but no thanks, Victor—knowing *your* sources. (*Angrily*) What you could find is my hat!

Baron (*exasperated*) I've told you—it's probably still with our luggage and the servants.

Baroness But where in heaven's name are they?

Baron (*faltering*) I don't know. We mislaid them at Charles de Gaulle.

Baroness Why?

Baron Frau Lurker suddenly needed the Gents and Ygor wanted something to suck on the plane.

Without them realizing a huge spider starts to lower itself over their heads C

Baroness (*disparagingly*) Humbug!

Baron Glacier mints, actually.

Baroness (*sniffing*) He should have used his thumb.

Baron Have you seen it?

Baroness Yes.

Baron (*sharply*) Then stop being fatuous. (*Before she can retort*) And cease
worrying about your hat. It's bound to turn up soon. (*Wryly*) Knowing
Frau Lurker, she's almost certainly commandeered the next flight out.

Baroness I hope you're right, Victor. That hat cost a small fortune, and I feel
quite nude without it.

Baron The small fortune?

Baroness The hat, silly!

Baron Yes—the fortune's *my* deprivation.

A bell tolls once. Glancing up, they suddenly see the spider

Baroness (*recoiling*) Aah!

Baron (*waving his hands at it*) Go away! Shoo!

The spider retreats up its web

(*Checking his pocket watch*) Ten o'clock. (*Turning to his wife*) Have you
given Cabbage his potash?

Baroness Yes—but the guinea-pig in him's chirping for greens.

Baron (*grimacing*) That's cannibalism.

*There is another eerie noise and Cabbage suddenly leaps out of the Baroness's
lap on to the floor*

Baroness (*hurrying to scoop him up*) Oh no, sweetie—don't! Stay with
Momma.

*He jumps out of her hands again and a mad little chase ensues during the next
few lines*

Baron (*moving to the doorway* L) Anybody here? (*He pauses*) Feel free to
gibber! (*Another pause*) Well that's promising.

He turns to watch as his wife manages to corner Cabbage UR

Baroness (*breathlessly*) Who are you expecting?

Baron I haven't the foggiest.

Baroness (*scrambling to her feet, clutching Cabbage tightly*) You mean you
don't *know*?

Baron (*shaking his head*) Neither who invited us, nor why. (*He produces a
letter from his pocket*) The letter simply says: "Take the diligence to
Bukovina; places on it are reserved in your name. At the gallows-tree—"
(*Turning to her, pointedly*) We'd have missed that, except for the corpse.

Baroness (*shuddering*) Oh, don't!

Baron (*grinning and glancing back at the letter*) "—my carriage will await you
and bring you to Borgo Pass. I trust you will enjoy your stay in my
beautiful home."

Baroness (*with conviction*) I knew it. We're at the wrong house!

Baron (*putting the letter away*) Elisabeth, we're *not*. (*Gazing round*) This place has wonderful character.

Baroness Which would be greatly enhanced by stripping it bare, installing sensible central heating, shag pile and a Heal's suite. But that will *never* happen.

Without either of them realizing, a bride of Dracula (the vampire, Ethel) slowly drifts downstairs R and slowly approaches the Baron

Baron (*puzzled*) Why?

Baroness The probability that the owners take *Interiors* or *Woman and Home* is as minimal as their use of a Hoover or Mr Sheen.

Baron Ah, but the glossy mag may not yet have permeated darkest Europe.

Baroness (*without looking at him*) What are you implying? That *I* counsel the unfashionable?

Baron (*turning to see the vampire; terrified*) God, no!

Baroness (*unaware of his plight*) The thought's absurd.

Speechless with fright, he tries to indicate the vampire, gesticulating madly, but she is oblivious of him

The vampire drifts off up R

They'd find my fees far too prohibitive. (*Turning to him*) Shall we sneer at the rest of the place?

Baron (*shaken*) I don't think that's terribly advisable.

Baroness Why? Don't tell me *you*'re scared?

Baron (*casting a furtive glance UR; bravely*) Of course not.

Baroness In that case, let's take advantage of absent fiends to have a real nose round.

Baron (*sighing*) If you insist.

Baroness (*firmly*) I do. (*Heading for the stairs, still holding Cabbage*) She who relies on the host never gets the full tour—if any. Let's go!

She starts climbing the stairs. The Baron glances round warily, then follows her

Baron (*wryly*) Onwards—into *mystery*.

They both exit

Eerie music is heard as the Countess enters from L

At the same time a grotesque zombie (Groat) enters up R in a lurching, uncoordinated fashion

Countess (*reading from her volume*)
> Presently my soul grew stronger; hesitating then no
>   longer,
> "Sir", said I, "or Madam, truly your forgiveness I
>   implore——"

Groat looks around the hall, moaning in a confused fashion. The Countess picks up the cat-box and gives it to him irritably

They travelled light. Now go!

Groat stares at the cat-box then lurches off upstairs with it as the Countess resumes her recital

(*Scanning the page*) Where was I? Oh yes.
> But the fact is I was napping, and so gently you
> came rapping——

There is a loud pounding on the door R. *She reacts angrily*

> And so faintly you came tapping——

More pounding as she heads up R

> ——*kicking down* the
> castle door,
> That I scarce was sure I heard you!

She turns and gestures to the door

> Thus I opened
> wide the door;—

The door opens mysteriously as before

> Darkness there and——

Frau Lurker enters the hall, goose-stepping, swinging a suitcase and singing wildly

Frau Lurker "Deutschland, Deutschland über alles!" (*Dropping the suitcase, she raises her arms triumphantly*) We have arrived. We are here!

The Countess exits smartly UR

(*Gazing round*) What a *dump*! (*Sharply*) Ygor! (*Whirling on her heel she heads for the open door and yells*) *Ygor*!
Ygor (*off; plaintively*) Help!
Frau Lurker (*staring upwards*) Gott in Himmel! What are you doing?
Ygor (*off*) What does it look like?
Frau Lurker (*grimly*) Swinging around, as usual. Come down—at once!
Ygor (*off*) I can't. I'm snagged on something.
Frau Lurker (*peering off*) Ja. It is a gargoyle.
Ygor (*off*) It's flaming horriboyle!
Frau Lurker (*sternly*) Do not urinate. It is simply a lifeless statue.
Ygor (*off*) This one isn't—it keeps hitting me. Ow! Leave off! *Help*!
Frau Lurker You have only one choice if you wish to escape.
Ygor (*off; eagerly*) What's that?
Frau Lurker Disengage the parachute.
Ygor (*off*) You're joking.
Frau Lurker (*shouting*) Ygor—I *never* joke.
Ygor (*off; glumly*) That's true.
Frau Lurker (*impatiently*) So do it. Schnell!
Ygor (*off; dubiously*) Oh boy . . . Here goes. (*Yelling*) Aaaah!

A crash is heard off

Frau Lurker (*chuckling*) The Ygor has landed. (*She marches over to the drinks table and starts pouring herself a brandy*)

Ygor limps through the door, clutching a large suitcase. He has an enormous hump

Ygor (*irritably*) Yes, but it hurt.
Frau Lurker (*sharply*) Don't whine! Forty feet is feeble.
Ygor (*askance*) Feeble? (*Dumping his suitcase* C; *sulkily*) Why couldn't we have flown Virgin?
Frau Lurker Balloons are unpredictable und slow. We could not keep the Baron waiting.

The door R *suddenly slams shut and they both jump*

Ygor How d'you know he's here?
Frau Lurker (*pointing at the floor*) See—footprints!
Ygor (*recoiling*) Where did *they* come from?
Frau Lurker (*acidly*) Shoes, Ygor. Those large prints are the Master's—size eight.
Ygor (*shrugging*) A lot of folks take an eight.
Frau Lurker Ja. But the smallest are undoubtedly the Mistress's.
Ygor Why?
Frau Lurker (*sarcastically*) They have a Gucci heel.

The sound of dragging chains is heard off and they both react

(*Sharply*) What was that?
Ygor (*tentatively*) A Teasmaid?
Frau Lurker Rot! (*Eagerly*) It was something dragging itself along the upper corridors. (*She knocks back her brandy and replaces her glass, peering up the stairs*)
Ygor (*wryly*) Nice.
Frau Lurker (*turning*) Nein—it is almost certainly *unspeakable*. (*She laughs maniacally*)
Ygor (*puzzled*) Frau Lurker . . .
Frau Lurker Ja?
Ygor Are *you* a virgin?
Frau Lurker (*sharply*) That is no question to ask a lady.
Ygor No—I was asking you.

She clouts him

Ow! Don't hit me. I'm black and blue as it is.
Frau Lurker (*savagely*) You will be a rainbow if you don't watch it!
Ygor (*recoiling*) Sorry. Sorry! (*He sits in the armchair, cowering*)
Frau Lurker (*proudly*) I, Brunnhilde Lotte Lurker, have given myself to no man. Und no-one has ever dared to force me.
Ygor (*wryly*) I'll bet. (*Puzzled*) But what happened to Mr Lurker?
Frau Lurker (*dismissively*) He died young.

Ygor Before you went to bed?

Frau Lurker Before we left the altar. When I lifted my veil, he screamed und dropped dead at my feet.

Ygor I wonder why.

Frau Lurker (*quickly*) He was allergic to bouquets.

Ygor (*nonplussed*) Oh. (*Brightly*) Didn't you ever fancy other blokes?

Frau Lurker Lots. (*Musing*) But there was only one who held the key to my heart.

Ygor (*rising to join her*) Crippen?

Frau Lurker (*glaring at him*) Der Führer. (*Bitterly*) But he was ensnared by that Scheisse bitch, Eva.

Ygor (*puzzled*) Gardner?

Frau Lurker Braun! (*Ruefully*) I fought madly for his love—but with a black eye, fractured jaw und concussion, what can you do?

Ygor She was a heavyweight?

Frau Lurker (*acidly*) She was slime!

During the following the spider gradually lowers itself over their heads C

Ygor (*curious*) How did Adolf take all this?

Frau Lurker (*miserably*) Sitting down, munching popcorn und cheering occasionally. I was mortified. (*Sighing*) All I could do was swallow my pride und dedicate myself to higher things.

Ygor (*knowingly*) Aryan philosophy.

Frau Lurker (*sharply*) The *Luftwaffe*.

Ygor (*wryly*) Cor—they must have been desperate.

Frau Lurker (*obliviously*) For pilots? Ja. (*Proudly*) Und once I had my wings I was the terror of the skies!

Raising her arms above her head she suddenly notices the spider. So does Ygor

Both (*terrified*) Aaah!

The spider retreats up its web

Ygor (*recovering*) What did you fly? Broomstick seven four seven?

She clouts him again

     Ow!

Frau Lurker (*fiercely*) A Messerschmidt, dummkopf!

Ygor Then why did we bail out just now?

Frau Lurker (*grimacing*) That was *Concorde*. (*Abruptly*) Let us reconnoitre the territory.

There is another eerie noise and both jump

Ygor (*reluctantly*) Do we have to?

Frau Lurker Ja. (*With conviction*) I sense a sinister presence here.

Ygor (*glancing up warily*) Only one?

Frau Lurker (*fiercely*) Und I am determined to seek it out.

Ygor (*plaintively*) Can't we leave it in peace? Maybe it's shy.

Frau Lurker (*rounding on him*) Dummkopf! The sensation I am feeling, the vibrations emanating from the bowels of this Schloss, tell me that whoever or whatever lives here is far from shy—und has *never* been at peace. (*Gripping Ygor's arm*) It has lived an evil life, gorging itself, like a filthy leech, on man's hatred, fear und blood—for centuries!

Ygor (*cheerfully*) Well, after that pig-out, it's probably sleeping it off.

Frau Lurker (*darkly, peering round*) Nein. The thing is wide-awake. Even as we speak, it is watching us—und *licking its lips.*

Without them realizing the vampire has entered up R and is drifting towards them

Ygor (*staring at Frau Lurker wide-eyed*) What are you saying?

Frau Lurker (*gleefully*) We are in for a fun time!

Laughing maniacally, she marches out L

Ygor turns, sees the vampire and recoils, yelling

Ygor Wait for me!

He belts out after her

Eerie music is heard as the Countess enters UR, still holding her volume of poetry. She and the vampire confront each other C, but following a commanding gesture from the Countess the vampire drifts off upstairs

Countess (*reading from her volume*)
　　　　　　And the silken, sad, uncertain rustling of each
　　　　　　　　sombre curtain
　　　　　　Thrilled me—filled me with fantastic terrors never
　　　　　　　　felt before——

There is a terrified yell from Ygor off L, then Groat enters L, chuckling horribly. He goes to pick up the two suitcases C

(*Impatiently*) Out, out—*out.*

He gives her a filthy look, then staggers upstairs with the cases

(*Resuming her recitation*) Well, then.
　　　　　　Now, to still the beating of my heart, I
　　　　　　　　stood repeating——

There is another fierce pounding on the door R. She slams her book shut in exasperation

Bollocks—*bollocks*! Why's there always someone at the door?

There is more pounding

It's like some infernal meeting. Four was plenty, now there's more!

She heads L as the pounding is repeated

(*Waving at the door, irritably*) Come inside.

As it starts to open she disappears out L

Isabel Channing bounces into the hall, swinging a small suitcase

Isabel (*loudly*) Well, hi y'all! (*She halts, staring about her wide-eyed*) Huh? (*With feeling*) W-e-i-r-d. (*Shouting off*) Harry—there's no-one here!

Talbot lopes in with a rucksack, dark stubble and pointed, hairy ears

Talbot (*gruffly*) What did I tell ya? This ain't Grand Central.
Isabel No—it's the *pits*.

She drops her case up C *as the door suddenly starts to close. Both of them react*

Talbot What the——!
Isabel Cree-py. (*Warily*) D'you think there's spooks?
Talbot Does a bear shit in the woods?
Isabel (*irritably*) You sure are a comfort.
Talbot (*pointing off* R, *emphatically*) You didn't see that thing swingin' from the tower just now.
Isabel (*faintly*) What was it?
Talbot (*unfastening his rucksack*) Hell, *I* dunno. It dropped outta sight before I could take a closer look. (*Wryly*) Not that I cared for one.

There is an eerie noise off and they both jump

Isabel (*shivering*) I should never have left the States. I knew this trip would be a mess the second we set out.
Talbot (*dumping his rucksack up* C) That tanker weren't bad.
Isabel Harry, it was *lousy*. So was that freight-train. But what beat all was hitchin' a ride on a sheep-truck! I've never felt so *cheap*!
Talbot (*innocently*) Well, maybe if you didn't look it we'd have done better.
Isabel (*bridling*) Oh, that's rich! It was havin' you on the end of a choke-chain that cost us First Class. You sure are unsavoury after dark.
Talbot (*urgently*) It ain't *my* fault, Isabel.
Isabel It ain't mine, either. (*Musing*) Though I guess when you get down to it—an' you had a wild time with those sheep!—it's my stars I oughtta blame.
Talbot How come?
Isabel The day that letter turned up I took a peek in the papers to see what I'd got comin'. An' you know what they said?
Talbot (*drily*) You'll be cover-girl for *Vogue*?
Isabel (*glaring*) No. (*Quoting*) "You will be obliged to spend money on an exciting journey to foreign parts in the company of a handsome young man."
Talbot (*grinning*) Well that don't sound too bad.
Isabel (*sharply*) It's what it *didn't* say that stinks. The trip cost a bomb—gettin' here was hell on earth—the guy I wound up with is a freak—an' where am I now? Romania's version of Elm Street! (*Furiously*) When I get home that liar won't be writin' stars—he'll be *seein'* 'em.

There is an unearthly creaking sound off and both react

(Startled) What the hell was that?

Talbot *(wryly)* Someone unwrappin' a Hershey bar?

Isabel Come off it! When did Hershey bars creak? *(She takes a small camera from her pocket, moving up* C)

The spider starts to lower itself from above

Talbot *(suddenly doubling-up)* Aagh!

Isabel *(warily)* What's up? You ain't on the turn, are you?

Talbot *(groaning)* No—it's my back. It's killin' me.

Isabel *(taking a flash photo of a coat of arms)* Yeah. That was a mean climb an' no mistake.

Talbot *(irritably)* The climb was OK. The mean part was you gettin' *on board*. *(Groaning again)* You ever thought of losin' ballast?

Isabel *(bridling)* See here, buster—compared to Twiggy I'm anorexic.

Talbot Well next time you want to go ridin' let me know—an' I'll order reinforcements.

Isabel I'll order you a *six-foot plot* if you don't dry up.

Talbot Oh yeah?

Isabel Yeah! *(Gesturing to her throat)* I've had it up to here with you dishin' me dirt. All along the line it's been the same old thing—"Let's kick Isabel!"

Talbot Aw, c'mon——

Isabel *(obliviously)* So what if I've got an appetite——

Talbot *(drily)* Like Jaws?

Isabel Maybe I do snore——

Talbot To beat Goliath.

Isabel An' I know I ain't soft-spoken.

Talbot Nor's Joan Rivers.

Isabel *(pointedly)* But at least I'm *human*. *(She raises her camera to take a photograph of him)*

Talbot *(reconciling warily)* Now hold on!

Isabel *(advancing)* I don't eat out an' order *Chum*.

The camera flashes and he covers his eyes

Talbot *(yelping)* Ah—no!

She pursues him up C. *The spider retreats up its web*

Isabel I don't cruise round on all fours—like *animated dentures*.

The camera flashes again and he ducks down behind the sofa

Talbot Get lost!

Isabel *(standing over him, pointing the camera downwards)* An' I definitely don't wind up lookin' like a *Mohair rug!* *(She takes several more flash photographs in quick succession)*

Talbot *(behind the sofa, desperately)* Ow-wwwww!

Isabel *(lowering the camera and stomping down* R) So there!

Talbot *(growling behind the sofa)* Damn! *(He rises and moves from behind the sofa, holding out hands which are now very hairy. In addition the seat of his jeans bulges prominently. Glaring at her)* Look what you've done to me!

Isabel (*askance*) What *I've* done? Ha! Those things are home-grown, Paddy-paws.

He starts to growl but is distracted as . . .

The Countess enters L. *She stares with fascination at Talbot's rear*

Countess (*wryly*) Is that a tail in your pocket—or are you just pleased to see me?

Talbot (*feeling behind him, startled, then embarrassed*) No—it's a draught-excluder. Who're you?

Countess (*moving towards the stairs*) My name is lost . . . Lost!

Isabel (*drily*) Tell us about it.

Countess (*emphatically*) No. I want to be *alone*.

She exits

Isabel returns her camera to her pocket

Talbot (*checking the length of his tail*) So do I.

Isabel Why? I'm doin' my damn best to be nice, Harry.

Talbot (*growling*) Baby, you don't know the meanin' of the word.

During the following Groat descends the stairs to fetch their belongings. The vampire also drifts from up R *to* L. *They exit shortly*

Isabel and Talbot are totally unaware of either

Isabel Then who was it who bailed you outta the Venice dog-pound, huh?

Talbot Just 'cos you needed the *map*. You'd have been stuffed without it.

Isabel An' I thought you were grateful.

Talbot Quit foolin'. You were thinkin' of number one—that's all.

Isabel (*blazing*) Well, that's a sight better than *doin'* it!

Talbot (*startled*) Huh?

Isabel (*jabbing his chest*) All those wheelchairs you watered—it's a wonder Europe's old folk aren't down with rust!

Talbot (*furious*) It's a wonder you ain't been *flattened*.

Isabel What are you drivin' at?

Talbot Put it this way . . . Do the words "selfish loud-mouthed broad" make any *sense* to you?

Isabel (*furious*) What do *you* make of *this*?!

She gives him a resounding slap and he reels. Recovering, he heads for her, growling and clenching his fists

Talbot That does it!

Isabel (*squaring up to him, fists raised*) Come any closer an' you'll be flossin' your teeth through your ass!

He hesitates, glaring at her and rubbing his face. The vampire and Groat have now disappeared from the hall

(*Staring round, irritably*) Now where the hell's my case?

Talbot (*grimly*) The Twilight Zone.

Isabel (*threateningly*) If you've *buried* it——

Talbot (*shouting*) I ain't touched the lousy thing!

Isabel I'll bet! (*Casting a last irritated glance round she heads for the stairs, then whirls to face Talbot. Pointing at him*) Follow me an' you're *dead*. Got it?

Talbot (*snarling*) Got it!

Isabel exits

He watches her exit then goes to sit on the sofa, tugging at the back of his jeans irritably, then frowning at his hairy hands

Jeez—what a mess! The Wolfman meets Superbitch. (*Glumly*) An' she used to be such a *sweet* kid.

Frau Lurker enters L

Frau Lurker So was the Borgia girl.

Talbot I guess so. (*Glancing at her, then reacting*) Oh man—all this an' Godzilla, too? What's goin' on?

Frau Lurker Nothing as yet, mein Liebling. (*Throwing herself on to the sofa beside him*) But do not fear—Frau Lurker's here!

Talbot (*rising quickly*) Why?

Frau Lurker (*following him eagerly*) The Baron und Baroness needed a bodyguard.

Talbot (*staring at her*) The Frankies are here, too?

Frau Lurker (*advancing*) Ja. Und if you like, I will take care of you. This Schloss may well hold all manner of unspeakable death——

Talbot (*warily*) You think so?

Frau Lurker Here's hoping! (*Seductively*) But I will see no harm befalls my fine, handsome und *sexy* young friend. (*She grabs him wildly*)

Talbot (*struggling to escape*) Great.

Ygor suddenly rockets in from L

Frau Lurker releases Talbot irritably. He is clearly relieved

Ygor (*excited; heading* C) Frau Lurker! Frau Lurker!

Talbot (*wide-eyed*) Not him as well?

Frau Lurker Of course. What did you expect?

Talbot (*drily*) Something better than this.

Ygor (*hurrying to shake Talbot's hand*) Mr Talbot! (*Feeling the hair he recoils with a yelp, then recovers*) You remember me?

Talbot How could I forget?

Ygor (*miserably*) A lot of folks do.

Frau Lurker (*aside to Talbot*) Wishful thinkers, mein Herr.

Ygor (*grinning suddenly*) But I never forget anyone. Especially a bloke like you. (*Gesticulating*) Those tufts—those tusks—and . . . (*Turning to look at Talbot's rear*) Oh yes! That funny little *tail*.

Talbot (*irritably*) Still the wiseguy, huh?

Ygor (*chuckling*) You bet!

Frau Lurker (*sharply*) What do you want, Ygor?
Ygor (*rubbing his stomach*) Food. (*Taking her arm and pointing* L) Let's get cooking!
Frau Lurker (*innocently*) What do you fancy?
Ygor Something quick.
Frau Lurker (*clouting him*) How about this?
Ygor Ow! (*Rubbing his ear*) Why d'you keep doing that?
Frau Lurker (*with satisfaction*) Because I like it.
Ygor (*plaintively*) But it's not fair!
Frau Lurker (*menacingly*) Nor are your *orders*. In this unholy Schloss it is I who lays down the law. Not you!
Ygor (*saluting madly*) Yes, sir! Sorry, sir!
Frau Lurker I should think so. (*Raising a fist*) Or else!
Talbot (*shaking his head in disbelief*) Jeez!

Frau Lurker marches Ygor across L *as . . .*

The Baron and Baroness descend the stairs, arguing furiously

Baron No, Elisabeth, I most certainly *won't* alter our accommodation. And that's that.
Baroness It most certainly isn't. The other rooms all have separate beds!
Baron (*with mock horror*) My God! Don't they know we're *married*?
Baroness (*brandishing Cabbage at him*) You're infuriating, Victor. And so is your sleep-talking. It drives me up the wall! (*Realizing what she's doing with Cabbage, she hugs him to her breast solicitously*)
Baron I've told you the answer to that. If you like heights—rig up a hammock.
Baroness Rubbish! If you didn't spout equations and formulae all night——
Baron I can't help having an active brain.
Baroness (*sharply*) Well, put it in a jar like the rest of them—and give me some peace!

There is a distant roll of thunder which causes them to stop arguing. They then become aware of the others

(*Delighted*) Ygor! Frau Lurker!
Both Mistress.
Baron (*staring*) Mr Talbot?
Talbot (*extending a hand*) Baron.
Baron (*taking it, then reacting*) Ah! (*Recovering*) I never thought I'd see *you* again.
Talbot (*drily*) Neither did I.
Baroness (*urgently*) Have you brought our bags?
Frau Lurker (*nodding*) Ja.
Baron So where are they?
Ygor (*peering round, scratching his head*) I dunno. (*Pointing to Frau Lurker, brightly*) There's one.
Frau Lurker (*clouting him*) Dummkopf!
Ygor Ow!

Baroness (*sharply*) Where's my hat?

Ygor and Frau Lurker exchange glances as Talbot stares round the hall in a perplexed fashion

Ygor (*sheepishly*) Gone, Mistress.
Talbot (*irritably*) Like my pack.

He starts to search for it, giving his rear a brief scratch as he does. The Baron stares at the tail-bulge, obviously bemused

Baroness (*shocked*) Gone? *Why*?
Ygor (*hesitantly*) I—chucked it.
Baron What on earth for?
Frau Lurker (*smugly*) He *chucked up* in it.

Everyone reacts with distaste

Ygor (*urgently*) I couldn't help it. It was a rough flight.
Talbot Turbulence, yeah?
Ygor No. (*Pointing to Frau Lurker*) She kept scrapping with the stewardess.
Baron Why?
Frau Lurker (*folding her arms*) She was stingy with the schnapps.
Baroness (*sitting on the sofa, miserably*) All that hand-stitching.
Frau Lurker (*emphatically*) All those *diced carrots*.
Ygor I don't know why. I never ate any.
Talbot (*wryly*) Nobody ever does.
Baron (*blithely*) Yet they turn up with monotonous—and colourful regularity.

> *More thunder as Isabel starts to descend the stairs*

The constitution of vomit is one of life's greatest mysteries.
Isabel (*with feeling*) Oh *p-lease*. I ain't eaten yet.

Everyone but Talbot stares at her in surprise

Baron (*nonplussed*) Miss Channing? This is—incredible. You're here, too?
Talbot (*sotto voce*) More's the pity.
Isabel (*glaring at him*) You'd best believe it, Baron. Though God knows why—an' *he* won't split. (*Staring round*) Mary an' Joseph, I never thought I'd meet the Munsters again so soon. What *is* this? The Creepshow of Ninety-one Reunion?
Talbot (*drily*) The Invasion of the Bodysnatchers.
Isabel (*sharply*) I wasn't askin' you, Mutley. (*Staring at the Baroness who is stroking Cabbage*) Why are you pettin' a vegetable?
Baroness (*simply*) Because he likes it.
Isabel (*askance, tapping her temple*) What about the bats up top?
Baroness (*pointedly*) Like your clothes-sense, darling, they need *lots* of attention.
Isabel (*bridling*) Now hold on——!
Baron (*sharply*) Exactly. If we're going to exercise our wit we might as well do it constructively. (*Pausing*) Now that we've all fetched up here—(*to Ygor*)—if not on a hat—the next thing is to discover who invited us.

Talbot And why he's run off with our stuff.
Isabel (*suddenly*) Say—maybe it was that dame in black.
Frau Lurker (*sharply*) Who—me?
Isabel No, sugar. Some other creep.
Baroness Who was she?
Talbot (*shrugging*) I dunno. But she sounded like Garbo.
Isabel (*pointing to the stairs*) An' she vanished up there.

Thunder rolls again. Everyone looks nervous

Baroness How odd. (*To the Baron*) Are you sure the invitation doesn't hold
   any clue?
Baron (*producing it*) I've told you—it's simply a set of instructions.

Everyone gathers round to peer over his shoulders

Baroness There's no signature?
Baron Not unless it's written in invisible ink.
Isabel Ain't you tried *heat treatment*?
Baron Yes, but it gave me hives.

She gives him a disgusted look

Talbot (*pointing at the letter*) Hold on, folks. What's that at the bottom?
Baron (*drily*) A neatly crimped border.
Isabel Above that, bright boy. (*Staring*) Looks like a couple of letters.
Frau Lurker (*emphatically*) It is!
Baroness (*exasperated*) Honestly, Victor, you should learn braille.

*Ygor chuckles, then cowers, seeing the Baron's expression. There is a flicker of
lightning and Talbot flinches*

Baron So, what do we have here? A Cyrillic C entwined with a D.

Thunder growing closer. More reaction

   (*Wide-eyed*) I wonder.
Baroness (*equally startled*) So do I. You don't think——?
Frau Lurker (*adamantly*) Nein. It is inconceivable!
Ygor (*shaking his head emphatically*) Impossible.
Talbot (*staring at them*) What are you sayin'?

A brighter flash of lightning and he recoils

Isabel (*wide-eyed and hesitant*) The Royals don't own *this* place, surely?

Thunder—louder

Baron (*delicately*) I can't say. I'd hate to commit myself before I spot a water-
   colour or a Billy Joel album. Have you seen any?
All No.
Baron Then my hypothesis is foundering.
Baroness (*shuddering*) This castle's a carbuncle.
Baron (*blithely*) In fact, it's sunk without trace. Chas and Di couldn't
   possibly live here.

More lightning. Talbot yelps and starts to bend down reluctantly

Frau Lurker But Herr Baron—who does?
Isabel Who else signs himself *C.D.*?

A loud thunder-clap is heard and everyone jumps

> *Behind them, an eerie light begins to flood the staircase as Count Dracula appears, then stands motionless*

Count (*grimly*) How about me?

They all turn and stare. Silence, then:

All (*with feeling*) Oh no!
Count (*smiling*) Oh *yes*. Good-evening, everyone.

Vivid lightning. Talbot howls and bounds behind the armchair

> (*Emphatically*) Welcome to *Castle Dracula!*
All (*terrified*) Aaaah!

Everyone tries to hide as a terrific thunder-clap is heard and the Count descends the stairs, moving to C. By the time he gets there the Baron has been pushed forward to greet him by his wife

Baron (*swallowing hard*) Count Dracula—long time no see!

He extends a shaking hand which the Count takes in a vice-like grip. The Baron winces in agony

Count (*grimly*) It has only been a year, Herr Baron. (*He releases the Baron's hand*)
Baron (*pained*) Has it really? My, how time flies.
Frau Lurker (*peering over the back of the sofa*) Not as fast as *he* does.
Baron (*with a cracked smile*) So *you're* our host. That's . . . marvellous. (*Turning*) Isn't it, Elisabeth?
Baroness (*moving to sit on the sofa; dismally*) Super.

Ygor and Frau Lurker emerge from behind the sofa

Count I am so pleased you and your menagerie managed to drop in.
Ygor (*scowling*) I'm not. It was painful.
Count (*glancing across*) You, too, Miss Channing and Mr Talbot.
Isabel (*acidly*) Don't mention it.

Talbot tries to stand upright

> (*To Talbot*) If I'd know he'd be here, I'd have gone to Hawaii.
Talbot (*drily*) If *I'd* known, I'd have told you.

Isabel starts to retort, then giggles, pointing to the short tail which now sticks out of his jeans. Warily, he feels behind him

> (*Angrily*) Aw hell!
Count (*staring at him*) I am also delighted you have arrived in one piece.
Baroness (*sharply*) A two-piece, actually.

Count (*surveying Cabbage*) With green accessories. (*Raising his gaze*) Shame there's no hat.
Baroness Well, really!

At this point Groat lurches in up R

Everyone reacts

Talbot (*wide-eyed*) Who the hell's that?
Count (*easily*) My manservant, Groat.
Baron Yes, but *what* is he?
Count A zombie.
Ygor (*grimacing*) Yuck!

Isabel sits in the armchair, wide-eyed

Frau Lurker (*staring, fascinated*) He reminds me of my husband.
Ygor (*askance*) Before the funeral?
Frau Lurker (*cuffing him*) *After*, idiot. When I dug him up to retrieve the wedding-ring.
Ygor (*wryly, rubbing his ear*) Lovely.
Frau Lurker (*examining her finger*) Ja—Das Rheingold.
Baroness (*to the Count*) What's happened to our luggage?
Count (*gesturing*) Groat ferried it to your rooms while you were—exploring. (*Smiling grimly*) I trust you have now gratified your curiosity?
Baroness Perfectly.
Count Excellent. I should have despaired had all your snooping, poking and prying proved tedious.
Baron (*joining his wife on the sofa*) What—with so much going on?
Isabel All those creepy cobwebs . . .
Ygor Spooky statues . . .
Baroness Weird wildlife . . .
Frau Lurker Und nasty noises . . .
Talbot Man—it's Disneyland! (*He sits down* L, *wriggling uncomfortably and flexing his hands*
Count (*suspiciously*) If you say so.
Baron (*cheerfully*) And if we *had* become bored, which is quite frankly inconceivable, we could always have entertained ourselves with a trip to the local tavern.
Count *The Stake and Mallet*?
Ygor (*wryly*) What else.
Count (*grimly*) Such a trip would have been futile, Herr Baron.
Baron They're closed for refurbishment?
Count They closed at sunset. If you had called at this hour—as strangers—you'd have been greeted with the darkest suspicion, and a salvo of silver bullets.
Baroness (*wide-eyed*) But why?
Count In this region, to admit an unfamiliar face is often courting death and disaster.
Isabel Well, with you for a regular I ain't surprised.

Count (*smiling*) My dear Miss Channing, I have no need to enter an inn to obtain refreshment.(*Licking his lips*) But there are many others who would—and their notion of pub grub does not include sandwiches or crisps.

There is a hideous howl off. Everyone reacts

Frau Lurker (*eagerly*) What *do* they consume?
Count (*emphatically*) Shepherd Pie and Ploughman Lunch.

The others all exchange startled glances

Because of this, all hostelries have become most exclusive—after dark.
Talbot Like Stringfellows, huh?
Count (*raising an eyebrow*) Even a priest would find it tricky to tipple.
Ygor What about me?
Count (*peremptorily*) They wouldn't throw you a beer nut. (*Musing*) In fact, on this night, of all nights in the year, the Pope himself couldn't sink a shandy.
Talbot Why? What's special about it?
Count (*grimly*) It is a celebration of evil. A time when the foul things of this world emerge from hiding and run riot.
Baron Just like an England away match.
Count (*sharply*) I am not talking about football, Herr Baron.
Baron Neither was I.
Count I am referring to *Walpurgisnacht*.

A flash of lightning

The Night of Terror!

Thunder rolls overhead. Everyone looks nervous

Isabel (*with feeling*) An' you've invited us here for that? Swell!
Baroness (*faintly*) The foul things you mention—the ones that run riot. What do they consist of?
Count (*shrugging*) Almost everything a nightmare can conjure up.
Ygor Freddy?
Count And friends. Creatures once human—others which never were. Monsters with talons, fiends with fangs—ghouls, ghosts——
Frau Lurker Long-leggety beasties?
Count (*nodding*) And things that go "Yum!" in the night.

Another hideous howl off

Baron Lord deliver us! But tell me, Count—and forgive me if I seem rude—your carriage didn't bring us here solely to provide a "meals on wheels" service for your cronies. Did it?

A pause

Count Of course not.
All Phew!

Count I invited you here for a variety of reasons—one of which is to face a test. A gruelling test of the survival instinct.

Baroness (*askance*) Not a whist drive?

Count No—a test of humanity's capacity to conquer fear and battle the forces of evil.

Fading thunder is heard

Isabel (*laughing*) *Humanity?* You gotta be kiddin'. (*Staring round*) I count at least five who ain't Mother Teresa.

Count (*evenly*) Which is just as well if we are to meet them on equal terms. Without our own special attributes we wouldn't stand—forgive me—a ghost of a chance.

Isabel (*fervently, to Talbot*) Then thank God for unwanted body hair!

Talbot (*growling*) Shove it, Isabel!

Count (*staring at him*) Yours is still a dog's life, Mr Talbot?

Talbot You've said it. An' it's got *worse*. These days I don't just change with the full moon, it can happen any time.

Baron But what sets it off?

Talbot (*itemizing on his fingers*) Headlights, strobe lights, neons, jewellers' shops—those cute miniature torches——

Isabel (*innocently*) Flash photos.

Talbot (*glaring at her briefly*) All kinds of stuff. (*To the others*) I'm tellin' ya—last winter in Chicago an' Detroit there wasn't a dry lamppost in sight.

Isabel (*pointedly*) Sure was "A *Tail* of Two Cities".

Talbot (*drily*) Ha, ha.

Count (*with feeling*) The same deterioration applies to me. I am constantly restless—forever flitting from place to place—and where I used to be particular about my victims, now I am promiscuous. No neck is unattractive. No neck is *immune*.

Ygor (*clutching his throat*) Master—did you bring a surgical collar?

Baron No. (*Morosely; to Talbot and the Count*) Nothing you say is news to me.

Count (*quizzically*) Really?

Baron A peculiar deficiency has been apparent in my household, too.

Count How?

Baroness (*pointing to Ygor*) Can you spot the difference?

Count His hump. It seems—larger.

Ygor (*miserably*) Thanks.

Baron As for Frau Lurker——

Frau Lurker (*menacingly*) Choose your words carefully, Herr Baron, otherwise tonight you won't be afraid—you will be VERY AFRAID.

Baron (*to the Count*) I'll say no more.

Count (*with a wry smile*) What about you, Miss Channing?

Isabel (*violently*) There's nothing wrong with me, thank God! (*She raises a fist*) An' if you suggest different you can suck on *this*!

Count No, thank you. (*At large, drily*) Well, it would seem the home team is stronger than I thought. One might even lay odds on it.

Talbot (*rising*) Yeah—but why's all this come about? This time last year I reckoned I was A-OK. (*Pointing behind him*) Now I'm the world's worst ad for Levis.

Count Perhaps we should look to the Baroness for an answer.

Baroness (*to Talbot*) Have you considered a kilt?

Count (*pointedly*) I am questioning the success of your last *soirée*. For it was following that that our relapse occurred.

Frau Lurker (*sharply*) If you think it was the food——

Ygor (*puzzled*) What food? You only gave them nibbles.

Frau Lurker (*glaring at him*) A nut is as gut as a feast!

Count (*interrupting*) Indeed. (*Turning to the Baroness*) But I rather think it was the *beer* that was suspect. Did you not promise us it would refresh all our unreachable parts?

Baroness (*awkwardly*) Yes, but——

Count (*sharply*) Then why hasn't it?

Baroness (*urgently*) The firm changed their slogan.

Isabel To what?

Baroness (*embarrassed*) "Only our beer can do *this*." And judging from what you've said, it obviously has.

Baron (*sighing*) You might as well have given them Theakston's Old Peculiar.

Count Quite (*Rousing himself*) Well, at least we have unearthed the cause of our misfortune.

Isabel (*brusquely*) *Your* misfortune, buster.

Count (*staring at her*) That's as may be—but now is not the time for debate.

Frau Lurker Why not? (*Giving Isabel a filthy look*) I know where my vote lies.

Isabel (*furiously*) Beat it, bitch!

Count (*quickly*) What I do suggest, however, is that you all retire to your rooms and freshen up before a late supper which, I guarantee, will be delicious.

Frau Lurker That depends on *who* prepares the snack.

Count (*graciously*) Of course, Frau Lurker. If you wish to avail yourself of my kitchen, feel free to do so.

Frau Lurker (*emphatically*) I already have!

Whirling on her heel, she marches out L

Count (*to the others*) And now, if the rest of you have no objections, I should like to speak to the Baron alone.

Baron (*faintly*) Is it a must?

Count Yes.

As the others start to move eagerly

One thing . . . Castle Dracula holds many mysteries—some of which are less pleasant than others. I warn you all—tonight you must not only look under your beds, but *in* them. You never know what you might find.

Everyone but the Count, Baron and Groat heads for the stairs

Talbot (*cheerfully*) Well, if it's some dame wearin' frilly knickers, *I*'m not complainin'.

Baroness You will, darling. It's bound to be Frau Lurker.
Talbot (*askance*) Oh man!
Isabel You're not sayin' laughin' girl buys Janet Reger?
Ygor No—*Ann Summers.*

    Frau Lurker leers in from L

Frau Lurker Und my last purchase was a whip!

    She disappears again, laughing maniacally

Isabel (*to Talbot, sniggering*) Have fun—brush-butt! (*She slaps his backside as they head upstairs*)
Talbot (*bearing his teeth*) Grrrrr!

    They all recoil before everyone, except the Baron and the Count, follow Talbot out

Groat (*shambling forward; swaying; guttural*) Wii thaa bee orr, sirrr?
Count Yes. (*Waving him away*) Back to your grave, Groat.

    Groat shambles out up R

(*Shaking his head*) Good staff are hard to come by.
Baron (*wryly*) Definitely.
Count (*curiously*) What has become of *your* valet de chambre?
Baron (*nonplussed*) Ygor?
Count No—the Do-It-Yourself job.
Count (*realizing*) Ah! (*Frowning*) I don't honestly know. He gave in his notice soon after our party, and I think he went to work at the *Ritz.*
Count The well-made serving the well-heeled? Admirable.
Baron My only fear is that with the reversal of the beer's effect and having to distinguish between Earl Grey and Lapsang Souchong, he may have—gone to pieces.
Count That would be disastrous.
Baron Precisely. Tea at the *Ritz* costs an arm and a leg, true—but no-one wants them landing in their *lap.*
Count Far from it.

    At this point Ethel, the female vampire who has haunted the earlier action, drifts in from L *and moves to drape herself against the Count*

Baron (*staring at her warily*) One of your hangers-on, Count?
Count (*nodding*) And a super barmaid, too.
Ethel (*pushing him away coyly; cockney accent*) Oh don't! You'll turn me 'ead. (*Moving to the table up* L) What are you 'avin'?
Count A brandy, if you please.
Ethel (*to the Baron*) Same for you, love?
Baron (*nonplussed*) Yes, thanks.
Ethel (*cheerfully*) Won't be a tick.

She pours their drinks as the Baron returns his attention to the Count

Baron (*awkwardly*) Well, now we're . . . alone—what do you want to talk to me about?

Count Something very important, Herr Baron. A secret which may present the solution to our cumulative misery. For am I right in assuming that you and your wife are just as tormented as the rest of us?

Baron What makes you think that?

Count (*as the vampire approaches with their drinks*) From the moment you arrived the castle walls have echoed to the sounds of your domestic disputes. (*Taking his glass*) Thank you, Ethel.

Ethel (*nudging him*) I made it a large one. (*She goes to hand the Baron his glass*)

Count (*to the Baron*) Love's young dream's a nightmare?

Baron (*shifting uncomfortably*) Yes. Although Elisabeth keeps stating she'll stay with me "till death do us part".

Ethel (*perching on the arm of his chair; warmly*) Ohhh—*that*'s nice.

Baron (*glumly*) Not really. She's notching up the days on the stalk of her umbrella. (*He knocks back a mouthful of brandy*)

Count Time is running out for you?

Baron Fast. There's only an inch to go to the handle.

Ethel Oh gawd!

Count I sympathize. For the Countess Dracula and myself life is equally tempestuous—equally bleak.

Ethel (*disparagingly*) T'uh! Weren't it always?

Count Not always, no. (*Sadly*) But lately . . .

Ethel (*to the Baron*) It's been merry 'ell, I'm tellin' you. (*She rises and moves up* R. *To the Count*) You should 'ave stuck with me, Vlad. *I* knew 'ow to make you laugh. But what did you do? Married a bloomin' snow queen an' dug your own grave! (*Shaking her head sadly*) *I* dunno. (*She saunters out*)

Count (*indulgently*) She's all heart, that one.

Ethel exits

Baron I'm sure. (*Staring*) So you and Ilona actually tied the knot?

Count (*grimly*) Yes, but we cannot agree who should hang who. I have no desire to swing for anyone—let alone La Belle Dame Sans Merci.

Baron *Ygor* will. Especially if there's a bell involved.

Count I do not doubt it, Herr Baron. (*He knocks back his brandy*)

Baron Where *is* the Countess?

Count (*waving vaguely*) Somewhere around—but out of sight—out of reach. My inability to conform to an acceptable pattern of set meals has led to an overwhelming disgust on her part, and an almost permanent remoteness.

Baron Yet you're still co-habiting?

Count In the most basic sense. She has the East Wing, I have the West. And there is a barricade in the middle.

Baron A *real* impasse, huh?

Count (*grimly*) Solid as a rock.

Wolves begin to howl mournfully off. The Count stands almost hypnotized. The Baron reacts nervously

(*Eerily*) Listen! It has begun.

Baron What has?

Count The wolves—the true children of the night—are serenading us. A hymn to *Walpurgisnacht*.

Baron (*grimacing*) Why are they doing this?

Count No-one knows. Not even I, and I have heard it innumerable times. It is a deep and dark mystery.

Baron (*nodding*) Like the appeal of "The Birdy Song".

Count (*coldly*) Like so many aspects of Transylvanian culture, Herr Baron. (*Glancing at his pocket watch*) And now, if you'll excuse me, I have an appointment to keep.

He takes his glass back to the table up L. *The wolf howls cease*

Baron With the blood bank?

Count (*smiling*) With my chauffeur. Today is pay-day. (*He heads for the door* R)

Baron (*sharply*) But Count—you haven't divulged your secret.

Count (*turning*) True. It will have to wait until later—(*grinning toothily*)— when we're all sharing a bite at supper. Besides, I am still awaiting one other guest.

Baron Who?

Count (*opening the door*) At supper, Herr Baron. At supper.

He exits to the sound of approaching thunder

Baron (*rising irritably*) How bloody infuriating. I hate mysteries!

Haunting music is heard as the Countess enters on the staircase, minus veil and lit with an eerie light

Countess (*pointedly*) "Quoth the Raven—'Tis sod's law."

Baron Yes, but—(*He turns to see her; astonished yet pleased*) Countess!

Countess (*advancing to meet him, hand outstretched*) My dear Baron.

Baron (*kissing her hand*) I thought you never set foot in this part of the castle.

Countess Not normally. But when I want to, I can.

Baron Despite the barricade?

Countess (*smiling*) It is merely a token of the divide which exists between Vlad and I.

Baron (*puzzled*) He implied it was inpenetrable.

Countess For humans, perhaps. But we vampires can overcome much greater obstacles than a pile of outdated furniture.

Baron I daresay. But what if he finds you here? Won't *that* present problems?

Countess Do not worry. Vlad will not return for some time. He has gone to feed his pet.

Baron I thought it was his chauffeur.

Countess He has trained it for many things. Gardening, laundry—massage even.

Baron (*smiling*) Many hands make light work, eh?

Countess Perhaps—but I find it revolting. Twenty hairy fingers grasping, groping or fondling one. (*Shuddering*) It's like some bestial *menage à trois*.

Baron (*grinning*) Well, the Count can't mind.

Countess (*disparagingly*) Vlad gets a kick out of disgust. If you explore the darker recesses of this castle, you will discover many more examples of grotesque fauna—some of which have to be seen to be believed.

Baron (*as an unearthly cry is heard*) I think I'll give that one a miss.

Countess (*quizzically*) But you are a scientist.

Baron Not any more. A year of adversity has diminished my ambition. (*Sadly*) I, Victor, Third Baron Frankenstein, no longer strive to amaze the boffins, topple established theory or astound the world.

Countess Why don't you write?

Baron (*emphatically*) I have. Penning my memoirs proved catastrophic.

Countess Why?

Baron I entitled them—*Genius in Bondage.*

Countess Oh dear. What do you do now?

Baron (*simply*) I knit and grow Bonsai.

Countess You poor thing.

Baron I am. How do you amuse yourself?

Countess I weep.

Baron Quaint.

Countess (*with passion*) Dear Baron, I am so *unhappy*. This year I shall be four hundred years old.

Baron (*nobly*) Three hundred and forty if you're a day.

Countess You are kind—but what's the difference? I'm so old I don't recall my star-sign.

Baron And that's why you're sad?

Countess No—although it's certainly worth a sniff or two. A much more potent grief besets me—and my tears cascade like torrents.

Baron (*glancing round*) I *thought* it was damp.

Countess (*fervently*) Since attending your party I have cried in every capital—watered the whole world.

Baron (*bemused*) Mmmm. But what has caused this lachrymosus? The beer?

Countess (*sitting on the sofa*) No. It was having to marry *Vlad.*

Baron (*staring at her*) Surely you had some choice in the matter?

Countess (*bitterly*) Unfortunately not.

Baron (*sitting in the armchair; astonished*) He hasn't dared to make you his prisoner?

Countess No, but *fate* has, dear Baron.

Baron How do you mean?

Countess Last year's hurricanes wreaked havoc in this region—and *my* ancestral home was reduced to a pathetic old ruin.

Baron (*flinching as thunder rolls again*) Well this is hardly Buck House.

Countess True—but here you only see the night sky through windows. (*Sighing*) And so I had no choice but to marry, make my habitation here and endure constant *misery*. (*She rises and declaims with feeling:*)

> Oh God! If only life were fair,
> I'd have a house in Berkeley Square—
> And sucking blood, which I despise,
> I'd ditch for Whoppers and French fries!
> But oh! This is a foolish dream;
> My life's a coffee—minus *cream.*

Baron Why don't you take up a hobby?

Countess (*sitting; wearily*) I have tried—but few things proved sufficiently distracting.

Baron Crochet?

Countess Mundane.

Baron Charades?

Countess Tedious.

Baron How about Scrabble?

Countess (*drily*) I leave *that* to the rats.

Baron (*as lightning flickers*) I give up.

Countess You are wise. The list of my abandoned pastimes far exceeds the national poll. (*Musing*) There was only *one* which offered some respite from self-absorption: taking brass-rubbings from the tombs of Vlad's ancestors who lie staked-out in the catacombs below.

She gestures to the floor. Thunder rolls more loudly

Baron (*wryly*) Sounds jolly.

Countess It had its moments. (*Bitterly*) But then outside forces intervened.

Baron (*puzzled*) How?

Countess (*rising and moving to* C) Three of Vlad's old flames came to stay.

Baron One of them being Ethel?

Countess No, these were younger, vivacious—still relatively undead. (*Furiously*) And they pissed me off!

Baron Why?

Countess Because once they realized *I* was the accepted, if estranged, queen of this castle, they determined to give me as rough a ride as possible. First they criticized my rubbings, saying: "That's nice—but you've missed a bit . . ." or "Real artists don't *trace* things"—or worse still—"I preferred the one you screwed up!"

She raises her arms in fury. Lightning flickers again

Then, when I told them to fade away or I'd have them evicted, they swapped shrouds for boiler-suits, formed a single vampires' action group and squatted the crypt. I couldn't get anywhere *near* it. (*Angrily*) Every time I tried, they showered me with mouldy nut cutlets!

Baron (*grimacing*) How unappetizing. Their reasoning?

Countess (*emphatically*) Vampires detest vegetarianism.

Another roll of thunder is heard as she moves towards him

Mind you, I did fight back. A month ago, in an attempt to dislodge them, I tipped a wagon-load of garlic bread into the cellar.

Baron Did it work?

Countess (*ruefully*) Unfortunately, no. The "thing" that lives there ate it all before the fumes reached them.

Another hideous howl is heard as she moves round his chair

(*Cheerfully*) But last week I *did* meet with success. I hypnotized a passing priest and got him to crumble a packet of holy wafers over their darling heads, while they were brewing a noxious bean curd.

Lightning flickers as she heads L, *almost skipping*

That put paid to their veggie vendetta. They fled, scattering lentils in all directions, and are now residing in a gypsy caravan, decked like Ophelia and reading each other's feet. (*She smiles with considerable satisfaction*)

Thunder rolls even nearer and a gale begins to blow

It's good to know the Church still holds some awe for the young.

Baron Indeed. And it's good to see you can still smile, Countess.

Countess (*startled*) Did I? Goodness! What could possibly have provoked that?

Baron A memory of a happier moment. Even if it was fleeting and—er—ever so slightly smug.

Countess (*sadly*) Can you blame me, though? Most of my happier memories relate to times and incidents long gone.

Baron (*nodding*) Mine too. (*With feeling*) And what joy there was in those first momentous experiences . . . Lying awake night after night——my mind boiling with fantastic ideas, my soul grappling with incredible concepts—it was ecstasy! (*He rises, lost in the past*) Science has done so much—but more, much more will *I* achieve. Treading in the steps of my masters, I will pioneer a new way, explore unknown powers—(*as lightning flashes*)—and unfold to the world the deepest mysteries of creation!

There is a terrific thunder-clap and the storm breaks outside the castle, wind and rain beating fiercely against the walls

Countess (*emphatically*) And you did.

Baron (*turning to her, shouting*) But it proved a total, unmitigated *bummer*. My ideas were faulty, my experiments went haywire, and now, to cap it all, I'm broke! (*Shaking his head*) If only I'd been Peter Cushing.

Countess (*advancing towards him*) If only I were *young* again. Whenever I fancied a quick bite I'd simply pop down to the fields and chase shepherds.

Baron (*nodding*) Those were the days.

Countess I still recall the fear in their young, innocent faces when I whispered: "*Hello*, boys."

Baron (*loudly*) Added zest—eh?

Countess (*bitterly*) Where can you find such youthful innocence nowadays?

Baron A crèche?

Countess (*shocked*) Baron!

Baron (*shrugging*) Well you won't find it in the Scouts.

Countess (*emotionally*) Oh, what am I going to do? Have you no suggestion to help me dry my tears?

Baron (*blithely*) Yes. (*Reaching into his pocket*) A tissue. (*He hands her one*)

Countess (*fervently*) Bless you!

She blows her nose and then both turn, startled, as a loud pounding is heard on the door R. *The gale fades slightly*

Baron What on earth's that?

Countess (*fearfully*) Something is out there!

Baron And not alone, judging from what I heard earlier.

The door starts to open and snarling and snapping sounds are heard; also a man's voice with a broad Scots accent

Jekyll (*off*) Down! I said *down*. Brutes like ye should be taught some manners. How dare ye greet me in this fashion. (*His voice suddenly becomes evil cockney*) Sod off, yer buggers! Else I'll *thrash* yer.

He laughs maniacally and the snarling and snapping fades. As they stare, an exceedingly wet and windswept Dr Jekyll backs into the hall. In his left hand he holds a doctor's bag, in his right a heavy walking-stick. As he turns to face them the door closes mysteriously. Outside the gale continues to blow, but moderately

(*Scots accent*) Foul creatures. Positive *animals*. No sense o' discipline. 'Pon ma soul! (*He drops his bag on the floor and stares at them suspiciously. Cockney*) 'Oo the devil are you?

Baron (*advancing, hand outstretched*) Baron Victor von Frankenstein. How d'you do?

Jekyll (*shaking it*) I'm fine.

Countess And I'm the Countess Ilona—(*with difficulty*)—Dracula.

Jekyll (*aside, cockney*) Bloomin' nobs! Never could stomach 'em.

Countess I beg your pardon?

Jekyll (*Scots accent*) I said—delighted to make your acquaintance.

Baron (*drily*) I thought so. Who are *you*?

Jekyll (*Scots accent*) The Count's guest, man. The Count's *guest*. (*Cockney, menacing*) Want to make somefink *of* it?

Countess (*delicately*) No—but what is your *name*?

Jekyll (*Scots accent*) Henry, madam. An' I'm a doctor.

Countess (*moving forward*) Well then, Dr Henry——

Jekyll (*Scots accent; irritably*) Dr Jekyll, confound it! I'm Dr Henry *Jekyll*.

The Baron and Countess stare at each other, speechless

What's the matter? Have I alarmed ye?

Baron } (*together; faintly*) Not at all.
Countess }

Jekyll (*cockney; evilly*) I should 'ave, though. I *should* 'ave.

He advances, swinging his stick menacingly. They both retreat

'Cos I might just tan the *'ide* off yer! (*Throwing back his head he gives an insane laugh*

Baron } (*together, exchanging panic-stricken looks*) Oh my God!
Countess }

They retreat towards the stairs as Jekyll continues to laugh, swinging his stick like a mad thing. Sinister music creeps in, growing steadily louder as

—*the* CURTAIN *falls*

ACT II

SCENE 1

Half an hour later

Powerful sinister music is heard before the CURTAIN rises. When it does, the music merges into a ferocious sequence of howls, shrieks and roars which come from outside the castle

The Baron descends the staircase irritably, his hands covering his ears. He is now wearing evening dress.

Baron (*shouting*) By all that's holy, will you lot put a sock in it! I can't hear myself *scream*. (*Wryly*) And I've a sneaking suspicion I'll be doing a lot of that before the night's out.

The cacophony continues and he advances to fling open the door

I said be quiet! (*Yelling off*) Why don't you gatecrash a pop concert? Do something constructive with your shrieking.

As he is speaking the Count starts to descend the stairs behind him. He, too, has changed for dinner

(*Pointedly*) There's no need to look at me like that. (*Producing a canister from his pocket and brandishing it at them*) I'm more than a match for hooligans, so clear off!

The noises fade and he slams the door. Turning, he sees the Count and jumps. The Count smiles. Distant thunder is heard

(*Gesturing to the door with false brightness*) Well, at least the storm's passed.
Count (*deliberately*) But another is about to begin. (*Curiously*) What were you threatening the neighbours with?
Baron (*awkwardly*) A concoction of Brut and Pagan Man aftershaves. (*He returns the canister to his pocket*)
Count (*drily*) Stunning. Will it keep them at bay?
Baron The majority. For the exceptionally stubborn strain I have the ultimate deterrant upstairs.
Count Which is?
Baron (*grinning*) Frau Lurker. She can drop-kick a gorilla into next week.

A scream off is heard, then the Baroness races downstairs, now wearing an evening dress

Baroness (*breathlessly*) Castle Frankenstein was never like this!
Baron (*shrugging*) It came close.

Baroness (*advancing to the Count*) Following your suggestion that we retire to our rooms, I went to take a bath. (*Wide-eyed*) But when I stepped in—I nearly died!

Count It can hardly have been too hot.

Baroness (*sternly*) No. Something revolting surfaced through the suds and started playing "This little piggy" with my toes.

Baron How childish. What did you do?

Baroness Forcefed it my loofah. (*Pointedly*) But just when I thought it was safe to go back into the water, something *much* worse materialized.

Count A Great White Shark?

Baroness Don't be silly. (*Wide-eyed*) A headless horseman!

Baron (*sceptically*) In the *bathroom*?

Baroness (*simply*) It was a dwarf riding a Shetland.

The Count and Baron exchange bemused glances

(*Sitting on the sofa*) It really put the wind up Cabbage. He took off—like spinach from hell—and now he's hiding somewhere, poor baby.

A yell, then Talbot races in from up R, looking relatively normal and pulling on a tuxedo

Talbot (*breathlessly*) Oh man—you won't believe what I've just seen!

All (*drily*) We might.

Talbot I was workin' out down in the dungeons when I met the most plug-ugly dame I've ever come across.

Count One-eyed and swinging a meathook?

Talbot Yeah. (*Staring*) You know her?

Count Very well indeed. She *was* Great-aunt Katharina. Did she offer you a massage?

Talbot (*grimacing*) With *boilin' oil*. I turned tail straight off an' winged a cannon-ball at her. (*Askance*) But she just stood there an' caught it! Ghosts can't do that, surely?

Count Not normally. But Auntie packed a great deal of muscle.

A scream, then Isabel races downstairs, wearing an evening dress

Isabel (*fervently*) I've seen some creepy dives, but this joint takes the biscuit!

Count (*sighing*) What have *you* seen, Miss Channing?

Isabel God knows! I just took a peek in the landin' mirror an' somethin' *gross* leered out at me. I couldn't put a name to it.

Baroness (*drily*) Insufficient make-up, darling?

Isabel (*angrily*) Dry up!

Baroness (*stroking her cheek*) *Most* unlikely.

Isabel Now see here——

Ygor suddenly belts downstairs, panic-stricken

Ygor Master! Master! *Help.*

Baron (*raising his eyes*) Not you, too?

Ygor (*desperately*) No—it's *Frau Lurker.*

Isabel (*sitting down L*) Is somethin' molestin' her?

Ygor (*askance*) Nothing's *that* stupid. (*To the Baron, urgently*) She's after a suite.

Baroness Well give her one of your mints.

Ygor A *set of rooms*, Mistress. First she invaded the bathroom, then she annexed the dressing room—and now she's out to occupy my *bedroom*. What can I do?

Baron Issue an ultimatum?

Ygor It won't work, Master. She means business.

Baron Then go back there, borrow my wife's talc and scatter it all over yourself and the furniture, shouting "Neutral" as loudly as you can.

Ygor (*scratching his head*) Duh—*why*?

Baron With any luck she'll think the room's Switzerland, you're Mont Blanc, and back off. The Germans have this strange respect for mountainous, snowy regions.

Frau Lurker marches downstairs swinging a dead rat and singing

Frau Lurker "Climbing over rocky mountain—skipping rivulet and fountain—passing nooks where Y-gor *quivers*."

Ygor (*groaning*) Oh Master—I'm done for.

Baron Not necessarily. (*Whispering*) If she goes flower-picking, cause an avalanche. (*Loudly, moving* L) Frau Lurker—do you like Edelweiss?

Frau Lurker (*coyly*) Only when *you* sing it.

Ygor and the Baron exchange bemused glances

Count (*sharply*) What delight have you in store for supper?

Frau Lurker (*stroking the rat*) A superb recipe of my Grossmutter's. A master race of culinary art. A truly memorable repast.

Isabel What's it called?

Frau Lurker (*shrugging*) Soup.

Talbot (*staring*) Any particular type?

Frau Lurker (*beaming*) Ja. (*Emphatically*) *Cabbage*!

They all recoil. She looks puzzled

Baroness (*tearfully*) Frau Lurker—how could you?

Frau Lurker (*sharply*) It would have been *water* without it.

She throws the rat to Ygor who juggles with it, disgusted, before kicking it into a corner. The Baron comforts his wife as . . .

The Countess starts to descend the stairs, wearing a stunning gown

Countess (*wryly*) Oh well—I'm sure it will fill a gap.

Everyone turns to stare

Baroness (*rising to greet her*) Ilona! How wonderful to see you again.

Countess (*taking her hands*) The feeling is mutual, dear, *dear* Elisabeth.

Isabel sticks her fingers down her throat and retches

(*Gazing round*) Meeting so many old friends at once is—overwhelming.

Frau Lurker Danke schön—but less of the *old*, ja?

Countess What can I possibly say to express my delight?

Talbot (*drily, sitting down* R) How about "hi"?

Countess (*staring at him*) I will think on it.

Baroness Your dress is fabulous, darling.

Countess Oh but yours is ravishing—a dream.

Baroness Isn't it just?

She sits again on the sofa. The Baron heads for the armchair

Isabel (*rising and twirling*) Well, my get-up ain't exactly dismal.

Countess (*staring*) True—but it still evokes a tear, Miss Channing. Does the word "fashion" mean so little in the States?

Isabel (*bridling*) Thanks a bunch!

Countess (*smiling*) You're welcome.

Count (*drily*) It is gracious of you to join us, Ilona. Or did you finally tire of manning the barricade?

Countess On the contrary. Thwarting your attempts to materialize on my side of the border provides permanent satisfaction. (*At large*) Last night, watching a vaporized Vlad filter through an accumulation of antiques, only to find himself imprisoned—genie fashion—in a discarded Perrier bottle, was a distinct joy. (*Smiling*) But not quite as gratifying as his picqued bat-squeak of "Eau shit!" (*Laughing, she sits next to the Baroness*)

Count (*grimly*) You are too harsh, Ilona. I was merely trying to offer you an invitation. Throwing me out of the oriel window was most uncharitable— and distinctly *shattering!*

Dr Jekyll stomps downstairs. He is now wearing evening dress, but still carries his bag and stick

Jekyll Confound it! Am I to wait all night for attention? (*To the Count*) I ask ye, sir. I *ask* ye.

Count (*graciously*) Of course not, Doctor. I have merely been seeing to my other guests.

Jekyll (*gazing round suspiciously*) An'a rum bunch they are, too—if I may say so.

Count You may—but I refrain from accepting the consequences.

Jekyll (*sharply*) Why? Are they a wee bit touchy? *Temperamental*? (*Glaring at them*) Can't abide temperament, d'ye hear? 'Specially if ye're *actors*. Loathsome insects, all! Never cease leerin', wavin' their hands an' spoutin' outdated rubbish. (*His accent suddenly alters to vicious cockney*) Get right on me back! (*To Ygor*) Looks like yer've got one on yours, me boy. (*Brandishing his stick*) Only one cure—one way o' riddin' yerself of the buggers. Beat 'em wiv a good stout stick! Beat 'em *senseless*, d'yer hear? (*Advancing on Ygor*) Stand still, boy! I'll free yer of the bastard! *I'll free yer!*

Ygor (*shrieking*) Master—save me! (*He hides behind the armchair, terrified*)

Baron (*sharply, to Jekyll*) You daft cretin! Can't you see it's a hump? A *hump*, man.

Jekyll (*still cockney*) Looks bloomin' thespian to me. I'm sure I've copped eyes on it before.

As Ygor peers round the chair

Does it ever whisper speeches to yer?
Ygor (*fervently*) No!
Jekyll Never caught it wearin' tights?
Ygor Not once!
Jekyll Or poncin' about in make-up?
Ygor Never!
Jekyll (*lowering his stick*) Hmmm. (*Staring at him*) I'll take yer word for it.
(*To the Baron*) But it could be *restin'*, eh? Simply restin'. If the bugger
makes one move towards a bright light, I'll 'ave it, d'yer hear? I'll 'ave it!
Baron Rest assured, Doctor, that's most unlikely to happen.
Ygor (*with feeling*) You bet! I'm going straight down to the cellar. (*To the
Count*) Pitch-black, isn't it?
Count (*wryly*) Yes. But so is the "thing" which inhabits it.
Ygor (*hesitating*) Then I think I'll just sit over there, thanks very much. (*He
heads for the chair up* R *and sits, hugging his knees*)

Jekyll watches him suspiciously.

Baroness (*to the Baron*) Darling, who is this—charming—gent?
Jekyll (*as himself*) The name's Jekyll, madam. Dr Henry Jekyll. (*Darkly*) A
name to conjure with.

The Baroness stares at him, horrified

Countess (*drily*) And possibly exorcize?
Jekyll I beg your pardon?
Countess Weren't you—or was it a friend of yours—the sensation of London
some years ago?
Jekyll (*grimly*) Madam—it was both of us.
Talbot A double-act, huh?
Jekyll Ye could say that . . . (*Cockney*) But if yer dare suggest the *theatre*—
Talbot No chance! (*Aside*) Jeez—what a nut!
Frau Lurker What *did* you do?
Jekyll (*as himself, proudly*) I transported science into society. I took an
incredible hypothesis, subjected it to chemical research—an' what
ultimately evolved was the true face o' man!
Isabel I knew it! You're a plastic surgeon.
Countess And you're dense, my dear.
Isabel What?
Count (*patiently*) Miss Channing, Dr Jekyll is—or *was* responsible for the
concrete manifestation of the alter-ego.
Jekyll (*pleased*) Well done, man! *Well done.*
Countess Through his experiments he devised a formula for releasing the
beast which dwells within mankind.
Isabel (*calling across*) Sounds sorta familiar, eh Harry?
Talbot (*growling*) Shaddup!
Baron (*staring at Jekyll*) A good man, under the potion's influence, would
become unutterably evil. Isn't that so?

Jekyll (*nodding*) Debased, degenerate—diabolical! (*Suddenly rounding on Ygor—cockney accent*) Yer 'ump, boy—did it just *twitch*?

Ygor (*cowering, desperately*) No—no! I *burped*.

Jekyll (*suspiciously*) Hmmm. (*He resumes his Scots accent again. With feeling*) The creature—for such it was—held no vestige o' morality. No scruples ordered its existence. (*Sadly*) The man who once walked proudly became a *monster*, roamin' madly. Madly! (*Gesticulating horribly*) He would creep about the darkened streets, stalkin' his victims with undisguised *glee*. (*He gives a mad little laugh*)

Talbot (*wide-eyed*) Oh man!

Frau Lurker (*sternly*) Be quiet!

Jekyll (*staring round at them all*) The prostitute on the corner, the drunken tramp in the alley were easy targets for his unbridled bestial malice. They fell unnoticed—unrecognizable. (*Sharply*) Except as a *pulp*. (*Giggling*) A ghastly, *messy* pulp!

Everyone reacts with distaste

(*Pulling himself together*) But the dregs o' humanity were not his *ideal* choice.

Baroness (*faintly*) You mean there's more?

Jekyll (*nodding*) *Much* more.

Frau Lurker (*eagerly*) Gut!

The others stare at her, disgusted

Jekyll (*darkly*) The aristocrat steppin' from his carriage—the army officer returnin' from his club—the genteel nanny wheelin' a wee bonny baby——

Frau Lurker (*rubbing her hands*) Ja? *Ja*?

Jekyll (*grimly*) Whether by blade or brick, strangulation or—(*he swallows hard*)—stick, these, his principal victims, perished hideously at his hands. (*Visibly brightening*) Then, come the dawn——

Talbot (*askance*) Are you tellin' me all this happened in one night?

Jekyll (*staring at him*) A night, laddie? Sometimes in an *hour*. An hour!

Talbot Cripes! He sure got about. (*To the others*) Makes me seem housebound.

Jekyll (*easily*) He was certainly what ye'd call active.

Isabel (*emphatically*) More like an active *nuisance*. (*Staring at him*) What happened to the guy?

Jekyll (*bitterly*) He was hounded mercilessly, because ye see, the formula had a lastin' effect. The beast gained more an' more control until finally he was obliged to fake his own death in order to evade the damn relentless pursuit o' the *law*.

Baron (*wryly*) Not to mention an angry mob or two.

Jekyll Ay, confound 'em! (*Wiping his brow*) Eventually, after an excrutiatin' exile in Wales, with nothin' but sheep for company——

Talbot (*grinning*) Oh yeah?

Jekyll (*glaring at him*)—he overcame the effects of his experiment an' once more entered decent society. But nae that o' London.

Groat enters from L carrying a tray of goblets ornamented with umbrellas, straws etc. He is followed by the vampire Ethel, who is carrying two dishes of marshmallows and pretzels

Everyone but the Count, Countess and Baron stares at her, startled

Frau Lurker (*recovering; to Jekyll*) Where *has* he lived?

Jekyll All kinds o' places. Mombassa, Bombay—an' heaven help me, Newport Pagnell!

Countess (*shuddering*) Doing what?

Jekyll Masterin' the secrets of Egyptology.

Isabel But where is he *now*?

Baron (*at large*) Another word for dense, anyone?

All *Thick.*

Baron That will do nicely.

Isabel (*bridling*) Am I missin' somethin' or what?

Count Several million brain cells, Miss Channing.

Isabel Cut the crap, bat-breath! Where's the guy—an' *who* is he?

Jekyll The answer to your first question is—here.

She stares round the hall suspiciously

The answer to the second—(*giggling madly*)—it's *me*, d'ye hear? Me!

Isabel (*clapping a hand to her mouth*) Oh shit!

Baron (*pointedly*) Am I right in assuming, then, that since you've emerged from—er—hiding—there's no more trace of *Teddy*?

Jekyll I'll be honest with ye—he does put in the occasional appearance.

Baroness Oh no!

Jekyll But ye needna fear. It's nae manifested in the *flesh*. Simply in the odd caustic phrase, aggressive remark or wee threatenin' gesture. Dinna concern yourselves. (*He suddenly rounds on Ygor, brandishing his stick. Cockney accent*) It moved, damn it! That was no belch. Did yer not 'ear its cunnin' mumble? "To be or not to be *thrashed—that*'s the question." An' I 'ave the answer right 'ere! (*He advances on Ygor*)

Ygor (*yelping*) No!

Count (*sharply*) *Please*, Dr Jekyll . . .

Jekyll halts, dazed

There are important issues in hand.

Jekyll (*rubbing his forehead*) Ye're right, sir. Ye're right.

Count (*indicating the drinks*) A cocktail?

Frau Lurker (*sharply*) Don't you mean *aperitif*?

Count (*grinning*) Those too, if you wish.

Baroness (*recoiling*) No, no!

Groat hands out drinks

Ygor But fangs for the offer.

Talbot (*staring at his goblet*) What *is* this?

Count A Transylvania Twist.

Isabel Looks more like Miami Beach. (*Sipping it*) Mmm—*awesome*.

Count And so is tonight's star prize.

Moving up C *he removes the drape from the mummy case with a flourish. Everyone stares*

Baron What on earth have you got there?
Count A sarcophagus.
Talbot Come again?
Jekyll A coffin, laddie. (*To the Count*) From Nineteenth Dynasty Egypt, am I right?
Count (*handing the drape to Frau Lurker*) Perfectly. It is the final resting place of the one history refers to as *Ka-Seet.*

Frau Lurker puts the drape up R

Isabel (*wide-eyed*) You mean there's a stiff in there?
Jekyll Ay—but a most interestin' stiff, d'ye hear?

Groat hands him a drink

Thank ye. Ka-Seet was one of Egypt's most colourful characters—an amazin' chap. Employed as table magician an' part-time sand-dancer by the Pharaoh Rameses the First.
Talbot Did he ever play Vegas?
Jekyll No, laddie. He was around long before the clubs sprang up.
Isabel So were a lot of acts. You sure it ain't George Burns you've got there?
Jekyll (*drily*) Positive. In fact, it was tryin' *comedy* which killed him.
Countess They didn't care for his jokes?
Jekyll Far from it. Most of 'em were real crackers—especially the mother-in-law variety—an' the Pharaoh couldna hear enough of 'em.
Count (*taking a drink off Groat*) But after several Royal Variety Performances his mother-in-law was more than surfeited—and one night, while consuming a post-show pomegranate, Ka-Seet mysteriously choked to death.
Frau Lurker (*nodding knowledgeably*) Poison—ja?
Jekyll (*nodding*) In every tenth seed.
Countess (*wryly*) Ingenious—if time-consuming.
Isabel (*sipping her drink*) He shoulda known pommies are bad news.
Ygor (*pointing to the sarcophagus*) What are all those funny pictures on the sides? Cartoons?
Jekyll Hieroglyphics.
Talbot One of Disney's buddies?
Jekyll (*raising his eyes*) Stylized representations o' scenes in the deceased's life.
Baroness How morbid.
Jekyll Not so, madam. In this case they are a record of all Ka-Seet's jokes an' tricks. (*Pointing*) This panel shows him sawin' a Nubian in two.
Baron (*staring*) Clearly for real.
Count (*easily*) The Egyptians were never ones to cut corners.
Isabel (*grimacing*) Seems to me they *were*.
Jekyll (*pointing again*) Yonder we see him dancin' on top o' the Sphinx.

Countess Fascinating. (*Pointing*) And there?

Jekyll (*chuckling*) Fallin' off.

Baron What do all the cartouches contain?

Jekyll Jokes. (*Pointing*) This one asks: "What d'ye get if ye cross an aged buffalo with a black scorpion?"

Countess I have no idea.

Jekyll (*chuckling*) "A poisonous old cow whom nobody likes."

Count Undoubtedly another jibe at the Pharaoh's mother-in-law.

Jekyll An' clearly his last. What follows is a graphic depiction o' the funeral rites. But I willna trouble ye with the details.

Groat places his tray on the table up L and the vampire Ethel now hands him the pretzel dish, which Frau Lurker immediately seizes

Countess Oh you can't stop now. This is riveting.

Jekyll (*sighing*) If ye insist. (*Eagerly*) The embalmers' first priority—to avoid the fetid stench of a corpse in decay, was to remove the internal organs.

Frau Lurker (*eagerly*) Ja—but be *specific*.

Jekyll While one fella occupied himself extractin' the intestinal tubes——

Talbot Looks like he's stretchin' pasta.

Baroness *Must* you?

Jekyll —another inserted hooks into the nasal cavity——

The Countess pinches her nose

—to pluck an' drag out the brain.

Ygor Yuck!

Jekyll Never easy—an' often callin' for the use of a wee straw to suck out the residue.

Isabel (*throwing her straw away*) Pukesville!

Jekyll All the soft an' malleable parts were then put into canopic jars.

Ethel (*proffering her dish*) 'Oo's for a marshmallow?

All Not me.

Jekyll The body, meanwhile, was soaked in brine an' embalmin' fluids for weeks on end before bein' swathed in linen an' placed in the tomb. The result of all this an' the passage o' time is a mummy, whose skin an' bones have become exceedingly dry, brittle an' salty——

Frau Lurker (*offering her dish around*) A *pretzel*—ja?

All No!

Jekyll —a dreadfully withered old thing.

Isabel (*to Talbot*) I told you it was George Burns.

A brief pause

Countess Well, this has all been very—illuminating—but what has "mummy dearest" to do with us?

Count (*pointing*) That sarcophagus, Ilona, contains more than a dessicated Cairo comedian. (*To the Baron*) If one of your servants would kindly open the lid . . .?

Baron Certainly. (*Gesturing*) Frau Lurker!

Frau Lurker Ja, Herr Baron.

Everyone gathers round as she opens the lid and throws it back. The Mummy is revealed, horribly decayed, amid a cloud of fumes. All recoil

Groat (*holding his nose*) Cor—whaa a pong!

Count (*grimacing*) Indeed, Groat. Thousands of years without a bath or a change of clothes has had a most unfortunate effect.

Baron Take note, Ygor.

Ygor Yes, Master.

Talbot (*peering at the Mummy's feet*) What's that—by his feet?

Jekyll (*awkwardly*) It's all that's left of his—um—er . . . (*To the Count*) It must have snapped off in transit.

Talbot and Ygor cover their groins

Isabel I'm gonna barf!

Count Fortunately everything else is intact. (*Reaching inside the mummy case*) Particularly this scroll. (*He extracts a roll of papyrus from the Mummy's grip and holds it up*)

Frau Lurker What is it? His will?

Count No. It is the means whereby we may all find *eternal happiness*.

Silence as they all stare at him

Jekyll Six months ago the Count sent me a copy o' yon scroll to analyse. It was fascinatin', d'ye hear? Fascinatin'. An intricate recipe for a most cunnin' product.

Baroness (*warily*) Not soup?

Jekyll No, madam. An elixir for perpetual jollity. A potion which enables the imbiber to face life with a permanent smile.

Baron I trust that doesn't mean rictus? I'd hate to finish my days emulating The Joker.

Jekyll I'm speakin' metaphorically, man. Metaphorically. The important element's the idea—an' with this in mind I set about distillin' the substance.

Countess Successfully?

Jekyll I'm sure of it. (*Grimly*) Though acquirin' Tana leaves proved tiresome in the extreme. They're as rare as sausage rolls at a bar mitzvah.

Count (*sharply*) But you did find them?

Jekyll Ay—whilst visitin' a herb garden in Cleethorpes. Luckily the owner thought they were a kind o' bayleaf an' charged accordin'ly. (*Opening his bag*) With these in ma possession, I then spent many hours grindin', mixin' an' simmerin' to produce—*this*. (*He produces a flask of colourless liquid from his bag*)

Frau Lurker But what are you going to do with it?

Jekyll (*impatiently*) Why drink it, man. *Drink* it.

A pause

Isabel OK then—go ahead.

Talbot Yeah. Knock it back!

Jekyll looks disconcerted

What's up, Doc? Ain't you too sure of it?

Jekyll Ay. It's just that . . . I thought one o' ye might——

Isabel (*quickly*) Think again, buster! *I'm* not riskin' life an' limb on some quack remedy.

Talbot Me neither.

Jekyll (*at large*) What about the rest o' ye?

All No, thanks.

Count We need definite proof of its efficacy first. And it would seem only you can provide that. (*Grimly*) So drink it!

He stands over him menacingly. A roll of thunder

Jekyll (*to himself*) God be merciful! (*To the Count*) Hand me a goblet—a *clean* goblet. Daren't risk pollutin' the stuff.

Baroness (*gazing round*) There isn't one.

Jekyll (*relieved*) Damn shame. I'll hae to forgo it, then.

Frau Lurker (*wiping her goblet clean with a tissue*) You won't. Use this. (*She hands him her goblet*)

Jekyll (*drily*) Most kind o' ye. (*Aside*) Blast your eyes!

Count Proceed.

Jekyll slowly unscrews the top of the flask

Jekyll (*gingerly*) Are ye sure none of ye will join me?

All Absolutely.

Grimacing, he pours a small measure into the goblet, swirling and sniffing it

Jekyll It has a remarkable bouquet. Remarkable. Care for a whiff?

Countess We take your word for it.

Jekyll A pity—because it's worth savourin'. (*Sniffing it again*) Och ay.

Ygor Get a move on, mate!

Frau Lurker Ja. Wet your whistle, Doktor!

Jekyll (*tetchily*) All right—all right. (*Raising the goblet to his lips*) Hae none o' ye a wee *guinea-pig*?

Baroness (*miserably*) We did have—an hour ago.

Jekyll (*eagerly*) Where is it now?

Baron (*glaring at Frau Lurker*) Inside a tureen.

Jekyll (*wrily*) Och well. For the sake of Auld Lang Syne! (*Lifting the goblet to his lips yet again, he suddenly whirls to look upstage, yelling*) God's teeth! What was *that*?

All (*startled*) What?

As they all turn to stare away from him, Jekyll quickly throws the contents of his goblet into the Mummy's face before adopting an innocent stance. The others turn to stare at him suspiciously, unaware of the new fumes which start to billow behind them

Frau Lurker *I* didn't hear anything.

Ygor Neither did I.

Count (*sharply*) Were you misleading us, Doctor?

Jekyll Me? Never!

Talbot Where's the potion?

Jekyll (*patting his stomach*) Down here.

Count Are you certain?

Jekyll (*bravely; upturning his goblet*) D'ye accuse me o' lyin', sir?

Count (*slowly*) No. But in the light of your initial reluctance I am curious to know why you've consumed it with such alacrity.

Jekyll (*blithely*) I was fussin' over nothin'. It turned out to be—er—most palatable. *Most* palatable.

Countess Do you feel any effect?

Jekyll Nothing as yet, madam. (*Pause*) Though—wait! I do detect a subtle warmth inside o' me. As if—ay! As if somethin' were *stirrin'*.

Eerie Egyptian music begins as a bandaged hand slowly reaches out of the mummy case. The Lights focus on it, but only the Baroness notices

Baroness (*horrified*) Something most definitely *is*. Look at that!

They all turn and stare as the fingers of the hand clench and unclench

Baron My God! The mummy! *It's come to life.*

Another hand gradually extends to grip the side of the mummy case

Isabel Jesus wept! How's it done that?

Jekyll 'Pon ma soul—I hae no idea.

Count (*grimly*) *I* do. The mummy, not Dr Jekyll, has consumed the elixir. (*To Jekyll*) Right?

Everyone turns to him

Jekyll (*desperately*) No—ye're wrong. Quite wrong!

Countess (*gesturing to the Mummy*) Then why is it *licking its lips*?

Jekyll I canna say . . . Might it be thirsty?

Count Most probably. For more of the same!

He steps towards Jekyll. The Mummy suddenly opens its eyes wide

Ygor (*terrified*) Master—*look*!

Everyone freezes. The Mummy shudders violently

Frau Lurker Gott in Himmel! What is it doing now?

The Mummy starts to move one of its feet. Everyone recoils

Baron Don't panic! Keep calm! It's simply——

The Mummy takes two lurching steps forward

    —*trying to get out*!

Talbot Just what *I*'m gonna do!

They all back away. The Mummy stares at them balefully, turning its head from side to side

Count (*to Jekyll*) You will answer for this, Doctor. Believe me.

Jekyll (*frantically*) Believe *me*—I didna know this would happen. (*Gesticulating wildly*) I simply jumped—turned—tripped—an' the elixir——
Countess (*emphatically*) Has raised the dead!

The Mummy suddenly utters a harsh, guttural sound

Baroness (*warily*) It's trying to *say* something.

The Mummy repeats the sound, this time louder

Baron Well? What is it?
Mummy (*a loud, grating noise—stretching out its arms*) M-u-r-r-d-e-r!
All (*terrified*) Aaaah!

> *Dumping their goblets as they go, the Baron, Baroness and Groat exit L; the Count, Ethel, Isabel up R. Ygor and Frau Lurker rush off upstairs, while the Countess, Jekyll and Talbot head for the door R*

Only the Mummy remains, swaying its head from side to side and moaning fearsomely as the Lights fade to Black-out

SCENE 2

Immediately following

When the Lights come up the stage is empty. A wolf howl is heard off

The Countess creeps into the hall from the door R. She advances to C warily, then turns with a start as the Count enters up R, equally wary. They link hands and then turn, horrified, as the Mummy emerges from L, reaching out for them

To the accompaniment of an atmospheric piece of "chase" music and a variety of crazy lighting effects, the following takes place with tremendous energy, yells, screams, ad-libs and the occasional appearance of the spider

1) The Mummy chases the Count and Countess upstairs
2) Groat chases the Baron and Baroness from L to up R
3) Jekyll (as Hyde) chases Talbot from R to L
4) The Mummy chases Ygor and Frau Lurker downstairs to L
5) A Spectre chases the Baron and Baroness from up R to R
6) The Count chases Isabel downstairs to up R
7) Jekyll (as Hyde) chases Ygor and Frau Lurker from L to R
8) The Countess starts to descend the stairs, then hares back up as Talbot, pursued by the Mummy, chases after her from L
9) Groat chases Isabel from up R to L
10) The Mummy chases the Countess downstairs to L
11) Ethel chases the Baron from R to L
12) The Baroness enters from R; the Count enters from up R and chases her upstairs

A brief pause occurs

  Isabel enters warily from L, *peering about her. As she reaches* C, *the Mummy emerges, also from* L, *and reaches out for her*

1) The Mummy chases Isabel off up R
2) Ygor and Frau Lurker, armed with weapons, chase Jekyll from R to L
3) Ethel chases the Baron upstairs from L
4) Talbot, holding a sword, chases the Count downstairs. Halting C, the Count turns on him. Talbot reverses the sword to make a cross. The Count recoils, covering his eyes. Talbot chases him off R
5) Groat chases Jekyll from L to up R
6) Ethel chases the Baroness downstairs to R
7) The Countess emerges L, Talbot R and Isabel up R. They meet C. The Mummy and a Spectre appear up R and R respectively. The Countess and Isabel flee upstairs, followed by Talbot. At the last minute Isabel pushes Talbot back down. Cursing, he hares out L, pursued by the Spectre. The Mummy lurches upstairs
8) Jekyll (as Hyde) chases Groat (or Ethel) upstairs from up R
9) The Count chases the Baroness from R to L
10) The Mummy chases the Countess downstairs to up R
11) A Spectre chases Ygor and Frau Lurker upstairs from L
12) The Baron, brandishing a revolver, chases Jekyll (as Hyde) downstairs to R. Jekyll exits leaving the Baron firing after him wildly. The Count enters L and the Baron turns and sees him. Terrified, he belts off up the stairs. Turning to the audience, the Count shrugs, then strides off after him as——

The Lights fade to Black-out

SCENE 3

Shortly afterwards

As the lights come up, snarling and snapping is heard off R, *together with a few muffled curses*

Jekyll rushes in, slamming the door breathlessly. Peering round the hall warily, he advances C *to pick up his flask*

Jekyll 'Pon ma soul—I didna dream the stuff could have *that* effect. Most curious. *Amazin'* in fact! Much more perky than Lucozade. I wonder if it's marketable? (*He suddenly goes rigid and conducts the following dialogue between himself and Hyde*)

Hyde 'Course, you'd 'ave to try it on a *live* bloke, first.

Jekyll What's that?

Hyde You 'eard. There ain't much call for revivin' the dead. The world's crowded enough as it is. No, mate—if yer want to make a bit o' dosh, try it out on a 'uman bein'. See what it does for them.

Jekyll Are ye suggestin' I test this on the others?
Hyde Yeah.
Jekyll It's completely unethical!
Hyde Sod that. It'll be a *laugh*.
Jekyll No!
Hyde (*evilly*) Then it'll just 'ave to be you—*won't* it?
Jekyll What?
Hyde I ain't wastin' no more time arguin'. Cop a load o' this, 'Enery!

Against his will, Jekyll starts unscrewing the flask

Jekyll Stop this! I tell ye, I willna drink it.
Hyde Wanna bet?
Jekyll No! (*As the flask is forced to his lips*) Damn ye, Hyde!

It tips into his mouth and he swallows some of the contents, gagging briefly. Then the flask is lowered

Hyde See—that weren't so bad.
Jekyll (*clutching his throat*) It was dreadful, man . . . I feel—*hewie*——!

He sinks to the floor, contorted and moaning, but gradually the sounds transmute into an evil chuckle which gets steadily louder. His hands clench and unclench convulsively, then suddenly he leaps to his feet as Hyde, grinning malevolently

Hyde (*triumphantly*) 'Ere's *Teddy*! (*He capers round the hall, laughing maniacally*) Nice to see yer—to see yer NICE! (*Another insane laugh. Gutturally*) See 'ow *you* like bein' cooped up, Doc. Tucked away wivout anyone to chat up—anyone to bash! Gawd knows 'ow I've lasted. All those years in the middle o' nowhere listenin' to bleedin' Taff sheep nearly did me in. (*Grinning*) Well now I'm payin' yer back, d'yer hear? Payin' yer back double. 'Cos you ain't *ever* gettin' out. (*Raising the flask in front of his face, he grins*) Now—let's see what this little lot does for the rest o' these geezers. (*He starts filling every goblet in the hall, chuckling—then singing horribly*)

> Roll out the barrel! We'll 'ave a barrel o' fun.
> Roll out the barrel! We'll put these *goons* on the run.

Finishing, he places the flask in his pocket

(*Evilly*) Now—where's me stick? (*Locating it*) Heh, heh, heh! (*He turns and sees . . .*)

The Mummy emerges from the doorway up R, *arms outstretched*

(*Alarmed*) Gawd strewth!
Mummy (*gratingly*) M-m-m-a-a-a!
Hyde (*backing away*) I *ain't* yer ma. Gerraway!

The Mummy starts to approach him

Clear out, d'yer hear? (*Raising his stick*) Else I'll do yer!

The Mummy keeps on advancing

(*Scared*) Mebbe I won't. Mebbie I'll just do a *runner*.

He exits L *at top speed, pursued by the Mummy*

A roll of thunder is heard, then Frau Lurker marches downstairs with Ygor at her heels. She is wearing a floor-length nightie, he a night-shirt

Frau Lurker (*adamantly*) Whenever *I* feel afraid—which is very rare—I whistle a happy tune.

Ygor (*desperately*) But I *can't*.

Frau Lurker Nonsense. Anyone can whistle.

Ygor Listen . . . (*He makes a feeble blowing sound*) You see?

Frau Lurker (*contemptuously*) Ja. It is truly pathetic.

Ygor (*quivering*) What am I going to do?

Frau Lurker Cower und tremble. Perhaps the Mummy will take pity on you.

Ygor (*hopefully*) D'you think so?

Frau Lurker (*shaking her head emphatically*) Nein.

Ygor (*ruefully*) I thought as much.

A scream—then Isabel races in from L *pursued by the Mummy. She is now wearing a short night-dress*

Isabel Help—help! Save me! *Save* me!

She races out up R *with the Mummy at her heels*

Ygor (*with feeling*) This is terrible.

Frau Lurker (*sharply*) It is *magnificent*. Everything one could hope for. Horrors beyond belief—menace in every shadow—und stalking us mercilessly, a lethal, creeping terror. Delicious!

Ygor (*wryly*) I'd rather have a cup of cocoa and a comic.

Frau Lurker Well you can't—so sucks! Tonight we are sampling the spectacular. Tonight—there is *blood on the moon*! (*She laughs maniacally*)

Ygor You've been peeking through the Rose Window.

Frau Lurker I have not!

Ygor You have. I *saw* you.

A yell is heard—then Talbot, wearing white T-shirt and shorts, races from L *to the stairs. He is pursued by Hyde, who is brandishing his stick*

Hyde (*singing*)   Teddy's gonna clobber a bow-wow!
                              Teddy's gonna clobber a bow-wow!
Heh, heh, heh!

They disappear up the stairs

Ygor You were watching Mr Talbot having a bath.

Frau Lurker (*after glancing around*) So what if I was? It is a free world.

Ygor (*grinning*) Pity you didn't get a free *feel*, eh?

Frau Lurker (*clouting him*) Dummkopf!

Ygor (*clutching his ear*) Ouch!

Frau Lurker (*passionately*) At least I wasn't acting the screaming nelly! (*Finding her goblet and knocking the contents back*) I have courage, strength—*willpower*. (*Towering over him*) I am a better man than anyone in this castle!

She storms towards the staircase, almost colliding with the Baron, who comes down wearing a smoking jacket and holding an open book

Baron (*drily, to Ygor*) Don't say it.
Ygor Why not, Master? She makes Rambo look *mimsy*.
Baron (*grinning*) True.
Ygor (*pointing to the book*) What's that?
Baron The Book of the Dead.

Hyde, stick raised, pursues the Count from up L to up R

Hyde (*singing*) After the ball is over—after I've *broke yer legs*!

Hyde and the Count exit

Baron (*to Ygor*) I picked it up from the Count's library.
Ygor What for?
Baron It's a set of Egyptian rituals—for departed souls. I hoped it would provide some method for combating the Mummy——

The Mummy pursues the Countess from up R to up L

Countess (*to the Baron*) Really—I never knew Hide and Seek could be so *exhausting*!

The Mummy and Countess exit

Baron (*staring*)—pacifying it, or——
Ygor (*helpfully*) Making it go bye-byes?
Baron Something like that. (*Sighing*) But it's totally useless.
Ygor Why, Master?
Baron I can't make head or tail of it. All these pictures of men, animals and weighing scales may well hold some deep, inner meaning, but to me they simply sum up life in a Cairo pet-shop.

Howls and cries begin off R

Talking of which . . .
Ygor (*nervously*) What's happening?
Baron (*drily*) The Grislies' rendition of *Eine Kleine Nachtmusik*. (*He heads for the door R, shouting*) So you lot are back, are you? Well, I've had enough nonsense for one night! (*He takes the canister from his pocket*) Open Sesame!

The door swings open and the noises grow louder

Don't say I didn't warn you!

Ygor knocks back his drink as the Baron flicks the cap off the canister

As he does, the Mummy starts chasing Talbot down the staircase to the door L

Talbot (*as he runs*) I don't care *what* you're after—just get off my tail, will ya?!

Baron (*sharply*) Hit the dirt!

Everyone, including the Mummy, does so as the Baron lobs the canister out of the door, grenade fashion. He ducks, there is a small explosion off, then the howls and cries fade away

  (*Rising triumphantly*) Victory is ours!
Talbot (*grimly*) You reckon?

  He rushes out L, *still pursued by the Mummy*

Baron (*pointing to the door*) Shut Sesame!

The door closes and he wipes his hands in a satisfied manner

  I love the smell of retreat—and this beats Boots at Christmas.

Laughing, he turns to Ygor, who has also risen and is grinning inanely

  (*Sharply*) What's got into *you*?
Ygor (*giggling*) I don't know, Master—but it tickles. (*He giggles again*)
Baron (*suspiciously*) Sounds like fleas. Keep your distance!
Ygor Anything you say, Master.

He spins round on the spot, still giggling. The Baron stares at him askance

  (*With relish*)   Frau Lurker once travelled abroad—ja?
                           And chased all the blokes till it bored her.
                           Then on the way back a sex-maniac
                           Jumped out of a bush and *ignored* her!
Baron (*wryly*) Is that a fact?
Ygor (*still giggling*) Yes, Master.

  He cavorts idiotically for a moment, then exits up R

The Baron stares after him, bemused

Baron (*emphatically*) The fool's flipped.

  An eerie light floods the staircase briefly as Frau Lurker begins to descend, wearing black leather and flexing a whip

Frau Lurker (*seductively*) Herr Baron.
Baron (*turning, startled*) Mother of God! (*Swallowing*) Frau Lurker, is—is that *you*?
Frau Lurker (*advancing*) Ja—mein Liebchen.
Baron What are you wearing?
Frau Lurker (*coyly*) A little something just for you.
Baron (*with difficulty*) But—why?
Frau Lurker (*cracking the whip*) I am in the mood for *lust*.
Baron (*recoiling*) Aaah!

She slinks towards him relentlessly

Frau Lurker   When the night wind howls in the chimney cowls, und
                     the bat in the moonlight flies,
                   Und inky clouds, like funeral shrouds, sail over
                     the midnight skies——

She pauses dramatically

Baron Yes?
Frau Lurker (*embracing him wildly*) It's time for *whoopee!*
Baron (*struggling to free himself*) Not necessarily.
Frau Lurker (*grimly*) It *is*. (*Seductively*) Up in my cosy love-nest, we'll be like
little mice.

He shudders

Und after we've popped some pretzels, you will not dare think twice. (*She
flexes the whip menacingly*)
Baron (*swallowing hard*) I believe you.
Frau Lurker Gut! (*Pointedly*) So—are you *with* me?
Baron (*desperately*) I—er—need time to—er—*consider* your offer.
Frau Lurker Very well. You have eight und a half minutes.
Baron (*puzzled*) Why such an odd figure?
Frau Lurker (*sharply*) It is the exact time it takes to polish jack-boots!
Baron (*faintly*) Ah.

She moves up R, *then turns*

Frau Lurker (*emphatically*) I shall be waiting, Herr Baron. Waiting with wild
und—(*cracking the whip*)—unbridled *passion!*

  Blowing him a kiss, she exits up R

The Baron, almost on the edge of collapse, hares to find his goblet

Baron (*fervently*) Heaven help me!

  There is a scream off up R *and then Isabel belts in, heading for the stairs. She
  is pursued by Hyde*

Hyde (*singing*)   Izzie, Izzie—give me yer answer do.
                                 I'll go crazy—*splittin' yer 'ead in two!*
Baron (*watching them go*) What in blazes is *going on* here?

  Hyde and Isabel exit

*He knocks back his drink as an eerie wind rises outside and a bell begins to toll
mournfully*

  After a second, the Countess descends the stairs, reciting sadly yet pointedly

Countess   Listen to the tolling of the bells,
                          The melancholic melody of the bells,
                          As in the wind they're ringing—

The Baron belches

And mournful notes go winging.

'Neath sullen skies, like hollow sighs
From iron breasts unsinging,
A tale is told of love grown old
And grief forever ling'ring.

O hearken to those wind-blown bells—

The Baron belches again, then his face freezes

Those tocsin bells—those tinker bells.
A dreadful doom their tune foretells!
The bells, the bells——

Ygor enters from up R *pursued by Frau Lurker*

Ygor The bells! The bells! (*Glancing behind*) Oh *balls.*
Frau Lurker (*urgently*) Do not flee, mein Schatz. I just want your *body!*

They race off up the stairs

Silence. The Baron's face takes on an inane grin

Countess (*picqued*) That does it. If I can't recite poetry uninterrupted I shall immure myself in a convent.
Baron (*grinning*) That would be an immense tragedy.
Countess For whom?
Baron You—if they insist on a vow of silence.
Countess Oh. (*Puzzled*) Why are you smiling so strangely, dear Baron?
Baron (*shrugging*) I don't honestly know—tonight being Fright Night and all that.

Hyde chases Ygor from up L *to the door* R

Ygor (*terrified*) Master—*help me.*
Hyde (*singing*)   Let's all go down the Strand—an' knobble an
                                        'unchback.
                            Let's all go down the Strand!

Hyde and Ygor exit

Baron (*waving as they exit*) You see what I mean? (*Imitating a ghost*) Woo—ooh!
Countess (*suspiciously*) Yes. Have you been drinking?
Baron A mere dreg. (*Passionately*) I'd much rather satiate my thirst with you, fabulous Ilona. Standing here, drinking in your sheer loveliness, is all the refreshment I require.
Countess (*dubiously*) I don't know—you'll probably need an Alka-Seltzer in the morning. If not *two.*

To the sound of a romantic tune:

Baron (*closing on her*) My darling!

Countess (*weakly*) You aren't aware of what you're saying, Baron. (*Quickly*) But keep going—I quite like it.

Baron *L'amour* looks every bit like *you*.

Countess Does it really?

Baron Absolutely. (*Standing above her*) Ever since we first met I've had this overwhelming desire to savour, to touch—to *hold* you. (*He does so*)

Countess (*feebly*) Don't! Stop! *Don't stop.* (*Suddenly*) What about Elisabeth? Won't she mind you seeing another woman?

Baron (*blithely*) She'd welcome such a diversion—to slip out behind my back.

The Mummy chases the Baroness from L to up R. She wears a négligé

Baroness (*sharply*) Victor—stop gossiping and do something!

The Mummy and Baroness exit

Baron (*as she exits*) In a moment, dearest. (*To the Countess*) *You* don't mind, I trust?

Countess Far from it. I've often been the other woman. (*Drily*) But generally not for long. My thirst is *easily* quenched.

Baron (*moving towards the stairs*) Well, I think I can promise you something—*substantial*—on this occasion.

The music ends

Countess Where are you going?

Without them realizing, the Count has stepped into the doorway up R and is listening

Baron Upstairs—to slip into something more comfortable. (*Grinning*) My room or yours?

Countess (*facing front with a smile*) Yours. Mine is rather dark—and confined.

Baron You're on. (*Blowing her a kiss from the top step*) Bin those hankies, Madame! Tonight you will discover ecstatic happiness!

He exits

Countess (*moving to pick up her goblet; to herself*) How very peculiar. How very—*stimulating.*

There is a roll of thunder as the Count starts to move towards her

Count (*evenly*) You are a constant mystery to me, Ilona.

Countess (*startled*) As you are to me, Vlad. Why do you persist in creeping up on people?

Count (*shrugging*) Old habits die hard.

Countess (*sharply*) It is not that simple—and you know it. (*She drinks down the contents of her goblet*)

Count Yes. No. (*Fervently*) I cannot help it. (*Pause*) I'm just a jealous guy.

The Countess suddenly freezes, expressionless

The Mummy enters up R, *arms outstretched and moaning*

The Count hisses and raises his cloak bat-fashion

Piss off!

The Mummy takes a back-step, then changes direction and heads upstairs

(*Deliberately, to the Countess*) How is it that, despite your vehement protestations that life's ocean is a desolation, I am perpetually finding you fishing? And your catch is generally *far* from a barren harvest.

Countess (*smiling enchantingly*) On the contrary, my darling Vlad, it's not every day I harvest a Baron.

He scowls

But your jealousy, in fact, defies me.

Count (*puzzled*) Why so?

Countess (*moving towards him*) You are and forever will be—the one and only one for me.

Count And what's that supposed to mean?

Countess (*simply*) My heart belongs to Vladdy.

Count (*disparagingly*) T'uh! (*He turns away from her impatiently*)

Countess What's the matter, darling? Do you doubt me?

Count (*turning sharply*) Quite frankly—yes. (*With feeling*) Suspicion torments my heart. Suspicion keeps us apart. *Suspicion.* (*Pleading*) Why *torture* me?

Frau Lurker pursues the Baron downstairs to L

Baron (*as he runs*) No—*no.* I flatly refuse.

Frau Lurker (*urgently*) But Herr Baron—*Houdini* coped with handcuffs!

They exit

Countess (*brushing the Count's cheek*) I know I was a naughty girl making you chase me across the globe all those centuries. (*She smiles*) But you have to agree—it was exciting.

Count It was bloody frustrating!

Countess Ah—but no man likes an easy lay.

Count (*forcibly*) Some *women* do.

Countess Don't be a silly-billy. There were others, admittedly—but frankly, darling, none of them stayed the distance.

Count (*drily*) Immortality gave you a head-start. By the time you'd said "hello" they were pushing up daisies.

Countess (*ruefully*) Sometimes before that. (*Glancing up*) But you scattered *your* oats with a similar vengeance.

Count So?

Countess We both enjoy a bit of slap and nibble—and in effecting peace between us we must acknowledge this. After all, it takes two to tango.

Count (*nodding*) It does indeed.

Dance music begins

(*Extending his hand*) Ilona.

Countess (*taking it*) Vlad.

They begin to dance. As they do so:

Whisk me off to paradise.
Count Any special place in mind?
Countess (*musing*) A mystic isle of fire and ice . . .
Count (*nodding*) Ah—Tenerife. That suits me fine.

Frau Lurker pursues Talbot from L to the door R

Frau Lurker But I will be as gentle as a canary. I swear it!
Talbot Tell that to the Marines!
Frau Lurker (*laughing maniacally*) I *did*!

They exit R as the Count and Countess continue dancing

Countess (*with regret*) So many times I used you.
Count So many times I used you, too.
Countess (*urgently*) But worse still, I *abused* you.
Count (*shrugging*) I get a kick from *being* abused.
Countess Seriously?
Count Sincerely.
Countess (*breaking away*) In that case, meet me in the ballroom in half an hour.
Count Why so long?
Countess I have to locate Frau Lurker's whip. When I have, come up and see me, *big boy* . . . and make me smile!
Count You can count on it.

The music ends as the Countess exits up R

The Count moves to pick up his goblet

(*Raising his eyebrows*) Weird! (*He knocks back the contents*)

Isabel rushes downstairs, pursued by the Mummy. When she reaches C she whirls, fists raised

Isabel (*fiercely*) C'mon, maggot-mouth. Make my day!

The Mummy hesitates. The Count suddenly goes rigid

Mummy (*eyeing her warily*) E-r-r-r-h?
Isabel You heard. One step more an' you'll be dressin' casualities! (*Tapping her head*) *Comprendez*?
Mummy Yerp!

Turning, he shambles out of the door L

Isabel relaxes, turns and finds herself in the Count's embrace. Lightning and a roll of thunder

Isabel Oh no—not *you*. (*Raising her eyes*) Someone give me a break!
Count (*tenderly*) Do not fear me, charming Isabel.
Isabel Huh?

Count I mean you no harm. (*With feeling*) I am seeing you, myself—*everything*
—in a new light.

Isabel Why? (*Glancing round*) Has someone splashed out on a candle?

Count (*wide-eyed*) This feeling is indescribable. Suffice it to say, it certainly
grows on you.

Isabel (*emphatically*) Like mould! (*Wrenching herself free*) Stay back, fang-
features! There's no way you're nibblin' *my* neck.

Count (*sadly*) That is not my intention. Trust me.

Isabel (*emphatically*) I trust *you* about as far as I can toss a limo!

Count Isabel——

Isabel Man, you're not fit to be human!

Count Isn't that stating the obvious? (*Pinning her in an embrace*) I merely
wish to tell you how fascinating you are.

Isabel God, you've got a dirty mind!

Count (*trying to kiss her*) Sensational—*glamorous.*

Isabel Don't get fresh with *me.*

Count After a thousand years? Impossible. But my feelings *are* genuine.

Isabel (*struggling free*) Yeah—genuine crap!

The Mummy chases the Baron from L *to up* R

Baron (*as he runs*) I've told you—you're not my type!

The Mummy and Baron exit

Count Show pity, Isabel. Have a heart.

Isabel (*recoiling*) If you're a donor, buster, hand it to the Baron. I want none
of it! (*She folds her arms resolutely*)

Count (*bitterly*) I warn you, Miss Channing—this is a decision you'll regret.

Isabel Oh yeah?

Count Indubitably. (*Thrusting his groin suggestively*) They don't call me Vlad
the Impaler for nothing!

He exits up the staircase

There is a fading roll of thunder

Isabel (*moving to pick up her goblet*) What a poser!

There is a yell off R *and then Talbot races through the door, bloody-mouthed.
He slams the door and leans against it, gasping for breath*

Talbot Oh boy!

Isabel (*sharply*) Where did you come by that blood, Harry? You ain't been
maulin' someone?

Talbot (*moving forwards*) No—I ducked into the courtyard. There's a mighty
odd tree there. Did you see it?

Isabel Yeah.

Talbot (*ruefully*) *I* didn't. Smacked into it good an' proper. Hurts like hell.

Isabel grins

We're never gonna get outta here. There's all kinds of things runnin' wild
outside!

The door R *bursts open and Ygor and Frau Lurker rush towards the stairs, pursued by Hyde*

Hyde (*singing*)   Come, come, I'll make meat pies of yer,
                                        down at the Old Bull an' Bush—
                                        once I've *skewered* yer! Heh, heh, heh!

They exit

Isabel (*watching them go*) It sure ain't Sleepy Hollow.
Talbot What are we gonna do, Isabel?
Isabel (*grimly*) Find a shovel, Harry. We're in *deep shit.*
Talbot Oh great!

Isabel drinks. Talbot wipes his face clean with the back of his hand

The Mummy chases the Countess from up R *to* L

Countess For an older man, you certainly do have stamina, darling!

They exit

Talbot starts pacing up and down. Isabel's face suddenly freezes

Talbot (*fervently*) There's got to be some way of dodgin' 'em all. The trouble is—whenever I hide they always sniff me out. (*Lifting an arm and sniffing*) An' my deodorant ain't exactly Skunk.
Isabel (*suddenly flirtatious*) No. It's a wow!
Talbot (*puzzled*) Huh?
Isabel (*advancing*) A real turn-on. Just like *you*, handsome.
Talbot Are you havin' me on?
Isabel (*passionately*) I'll have you *anywhere.* Just say when!

The Baron pursues the Baroness from up R *to* L

Baroness (*firmly*) Not tonight, Victor. I have a headache.
Baron (*desperately*) Elisabeth!

The Baron and Baroness exit

Talbot (*staring after them*) What the hell's got into everyone?
Isabel I dunno. But it sure is wonderful! (*Spinning round, caressing herself*) Harry, I feel pretty. Truly pretty! I feel witty, charming—gay!

Talbot stares at her askance

And so—*sensual.*
Talbot (*sharply*) Feel what you like—but make sure it ain't me.
Isabel (*scowling*) Spoilsport! (*Coyly*) I thought you'd enjoy me bein' kind to a four-legged friend?
Talbot Well, if you fancy savin' wildlife, go out there—(*pointing* R) an' do it. It's like Noah's Ark on shore leave.
Isabel (*picqued*) Mebbe I will. You're sure no fun. (*She heads for the door, then turns; provocatively*) But if you change your mind—remember, Harry, I'm just a girl who can't say *no.*

She exits

Talbot sits on the sofa, scowling

Talbot You did—an' *often*. The most negative chick I ever met.

There is a scream off L and then the Baroness races in to C. Despite her négligé she still wears her jewellery

Baroness (*exasperated*) Honestly—things are bad enough here without being pursued by an overgrown loo-roll! (*She moves to pick up her goblet*)
Talbot (*nodding*) Pretty grim, huh?
Baroness Positively perverse. (*Shuddering*) Thank God we're not in Kensington. I'd *never* live it down. (*She drinks*)

The Countess and the Baron race in from L and head up R

Countess (*as they go*) And to think Oedipus *loved* his mummy.
Baron (*drily*) That was different.
Talbot (*staring*) Can't the Baron think up something?

The Baron and Countess exit

Baroness *Victor*? Don't make me laugh! He'd probably recycle the Mummy into papyrus notepaper—and that could take weeks. (*She suddenly shivers from head to foot, then stares at Talbot with undisguised interest*) If only he was more like you, Harry.
Talbot In what way?
Baroness (*moving closer*) Oh, how shall I put it? With your laconic charm . . . Resolute masculinity . . . (*Licking her lips*) New World *physique*. May I sit?
Talbot (*nonplussed*) Feel free.
Baroness Thank you. (*She plumps herself in his lap. Seductively*) What big eyes you have.
Talbot (*awkwardly*) A lot of folks say that.
Baroness (*pinching his arm*) Such strong arms, too.
Talbot (*wincing*) They ain't bad.
Baroness (*gripping his leg*) And your *thighs* . . .
Talbot (*warily*) Now hold on!
Baroness (*eagerly*) I am! I truly *admire* a man with a good pair of legs.
Talbot (*brusquely*) Then stick to hubby. He's got a real collection!
Baroness But not *live* ones, like yours.
Talbot Don't be too sure. One of mine's just given up the ghost. Can you shift slightly?
Baroness In which direction?
Talbot Off!
Baroness (*piqued*) Very well. (*She slides to sit next to him*)

The Mummy enters silently from L and gradually crosses to R behind them

(*Examining her nails*) Bored, bored, *bored*! (*Suddenly*) Would you like to snog?
Talbot (*askance*) What?
Baroness Good! (*She pins him with a passionate kiss*)

Talbot (*struggling free*) Hey—cut that out!
Baroness Why? Don't you like it?
Talbot Sure—but I ain't the type a lady should mess with.
Baroness Your modesty's commendable. (*Raunchy*) But this lady's a *tramp*!

She jumps on him again as the Mummy opens the door R

Talbot (*struggling*) No! You know *my* problem——
Mummy (*bleating loudly as it exits*) B-a-a-a!

   The Mummy exits

Talbot (*jumping to his feet*) So I find sheep cute. But that don't mean——
Baroness (*quickly*) *I* didn't say it.
Talbot (*gesturing at the empty hall*) Then who did? (*Glowering at her, he goes to pick up his goblet*)
Baroness (*rising; placatory*) Harry . . .
Talbot (*sharply*) 'Nuff said, eh? (*He drinks, shudders violently, then replaces the goblet*)
Baroness Agreed. (*Wildly*) Now let's see some *action*!

She pulls him down on to the sofa again as . . .

   Frau Lurker pursues the Count downstairs to the doorway up R

Frau Lurker Ja! Ja! I'm just a *vampire* for your love. Come back, Vlad!
Count (*fervently*) No way, ducky!

   They exit

The Baroness is tugging off Talbot's trainers

Talbot (*amused*) What are you doin'?
Baroness (*gleefully*) These shoes were made for walking—but now they're going to *fly*. (*Giggling, she throws them out of the doorway* L)

   The Mummy chases Isabel from R *to up* R

Isabel Catch me if you can, bandage-butt. Last one to the library's a sissy!

   They exit

Talbot (*trying to see what's happening*) What the——
Baroness (*pinning him down again*) Wild thing—I think I *love* you!
Talbot (*as she tries to remove his T-shirt*) Oh yeah!

Hyde pursues Ygor downstairs to the doorway up R

Hyde (*singing*)   You made me *bash* yer. I really love to do it.
                    Yer *know* I love to do it!
Ygor (*terrified*) Yes—yes! *Help*!

   They exit

A wolf howl is heard and Talbot contorts violently

Talbot (*pained*) Oh no!

Baroness (*releasing him; startled*) What's wrong?

Talbot (*sitting up with difficulty*) Mates of mine have come callin'.

Baroness (*as another howl is heard*) Good heavens!

Talbot (*leaning forward, grimacing*) An' I've a feelin'—ugh!—I'll soon be . . . joining 'em.

Baroness (*rising; emphatically*) Oh no you won't!

As Talbot clutches the small of his back, growling with pain, she marches over to the door R *and flings it open*

(*Shouting off*) Harry won't be out tonight—he's got chores to do! (*She slams the door shut and returns to* C)

Talbot (*grimacing*) That won't stop 'em. Nor *me*, when it comes down to it. (*He bends forward, clenching his hands*) You'd best leave me, lady. (*Growling*) Leave me *now*!

Baroness (*folding her arms*) No.

Talbot You've gotta!

Baroness Give me one good reason.

Talbot (*askance*) Can't you see I'm *changin'*? (*He holds out hands which have crooked fingers*) I'm turnin' into a goddamn *wolf*! (*He throws back his head and howls*)

Baroness (*impassively*) Don't be ridiculous?

Talbot (*nonplussed*) Huh?

Baroness (*gesturing*) For one, there's no moon . . .

Talbot (*growling*) That don't mean nothin'. (*Pointing*) It's those diamonds of yours catchin' the candles!

Baroness Oh, how *feeble*.

Talbot I'm tellin' ya, lady——

Baroness (*emphatically*) Take a good look at yourself.

As he hesitates

You're no different than you were before.

Talbot (*doubtfully*) You sure?

Baroness (*drily*) A mite tetchy, perhaps, but——

Talbot (*checking his arms and legs*) There's no *fur*?

Baroness None that I can see.

Talbot (*touching his nose*) My nose ain't grown any?

Baroness No.

Talbot (*opening his mouth*) How about my teeth?

Baroness Just perfect.

Talbot (*relieved*) Hallelujah! (*Frowning*) But I don't get it. Those sure felt like—growin' pains.

Another wolf howl is heard and he shudders briefly

Baroness (*smiling*) Not a bit of it. They were all in your mind. (*Holding out her hand to him*) Come here, you silly pup!

He rises, grinning sheepishly, unaware of the large bushy tail which sticks out behind him. So is she

Talbot (*hitching up his shorts; suggestively*) So—er—where were we?

Before she can reply Hyde saunters in from up R, *swinging his stick*

They separate as he moves towards them

Hyde (*singing*)   'Ow much is that doggy by the sofa?
                              The one wiv the waggly tail . . .
Talbot (*aggressively*) Eat my shorts!

Hyde jabs a finger in the direction of Talbot's rear, grinning, as . . .

Groat sidles in from L

Talbot explores the back of his shorts warily

Hyde (*raising his stick*)   'Ow much is that doggy by the sofa?
Talbot (*discovering his tail; exasperated*) Oh *man*!

The Baroness claps a hand to her mouth, giggling

Hyde (*villainously*)   Oh let's watch the doggy get *nailed*!

Before Talbot realizes what's happening Hyde gives him a sharp tap on the head with his stick and he falls unconscious into Groat's arms. Hyde signals him to drag Talbot out L *and drops his stick on the sofa*

     (*Evilly*) Heh, heh, heh!

     Groat exits with Talbot

Baroness (*horrified*) What did you do that for?
Hyde (*advancing towards her, casually*) So you an' I could 'ave a little chat.
Baroness (*staring*) Who *are* you?
Hyde (*dusting his hands, grinning*) Well I ain't Burlington Bertie, an' that's a fact. (*Pause*) I *was* the adorable Dr Jekyll—now I'm the 'ateful Mister 'Yde! Heh, heh, heh!
Baroness (*recoiling*) Oh no!
Hyde (*leering*) Oh *yes*. (*Gripping her arm*) Now don't yer dare do a bunk. Not till I've 'ad a word wiv yer . . . (*Grinning*) Mebbe not even *then*.
Baroness Let me go! (*She struggles*)
Hyde Whoa, Beauty! *Whoa.* You needs a bit o' breakin' in.
Baroness (*sharply*) I am not a *horse*.
Hyde (*grinning*) Ain't yer? I knows a good filly when I sees one.
Baroness (*slapping him*) How dare you!
Hyde (*pleased*) Cor! I likes a woman wiv pluck. It makes me mouf water. (*He licks his lips lasciviously*)
Baroness (*shuddering*) How vulgar—after Ascot. (*Haughtily*) Don't you know, man—I'm a Baroness.
Hyde Oh yes, ma'am. *Oh yes.* All the more appetizin'!

She screams

     Sinister music is heard as the Mummy enters from up R, *arms outstretched*

Mummy (*threateningly*) M-a-a-a-h!

Hyde (*turning*) I've told yer before—I'm nuffink *like* yer ma. Get out o' here!

As the Mummy continues to advance Hyde is forced to release the Baroness. She retreats into a corner, wide-eyed

(*Rushing to find his stick*) I'm warnin' yer . . . Come any closer an' I'll smash yer 'ead in. Smash it to bits!

The Mummy keeps on approaching him

(*Raising his stick*) Right—yer've asked for this!

He attempts to clobber the Mummy, but instead finds himself disarmed and seized by the throat

(*Choking*) Aaah!

The Mummy shakes him until he goes limp and lets him slide to the floor. The music ends

Mummy (*raising its arms triumphantly*) K-a-a-a!

Ethel enters up R, *Groat* L

The Mummy moans, pointing at Hyde then the mummy case. The two of them advance and drag the inert body up C. *Heaving it upright, they then lock it inside the case. The Mummy turns to the Baroness who is watching them all fearfully*

(*Staring at her, its head on one side*) M-u-h?
Baroness (*desperately*) Don't you dare come near me!

It does and she flees up C

(*To herself*) What can I do?

Searching for a weapon, she is obliged to resort to the dish of marshmallows which Ethel hands to her nonchalantly. One by one she throws them at the advancing Mummy

Stay back! Leave me alone!

It refuses to do so and she turns to Ethel and Groat, pleading

Someone *help* me.

Groat nudges Ethel and she reaches out to take the now empty dish from the Baroness, who stares at them in disbelief before turning to see the Mummy next to her. It reaches out to touch her

No!

It clasps her in its arms and she immediately faints. The Mummy picks her up and carries her to the sofa, laying her across it. It then turns to Ethel, moaning and gesturing to one of the weapons on the walls—an ornamental knife. She goes to fetch it as Egyptian music is heard: something suitable for a magic act. Having been handed the knife the Mummy raises it, point downwards, over the Baroness's breast. As the Lights focus on this tableau . . .

Everyone off-stage but Talbot hurries into the hall. (Ygor's hump is now missing) Seeing the Mummy and Baroness they all freeze

Baron (*askance*) What in heaven's name——?
Frau Lurker (*excited*) A sacrifice. (*Clapping*) Wunderbar!
Countess (*horrified*) But what's he going to do?
Isabel What d'you think? He's gonna stick that *knife* through her.
Frau Lurker (*eagerly*) Any second now!
Baroness (*stirring*) Victor—help me! Don't let him——

The knife plunges into her breast and she screams. The others turn away, apart from Frau Lurker, covering their eyes. The Mummy extracts the knife, then raises it again

Baron (*turning back*) Elisabeth . . . darling! Are you all right?
Baroness I—I don't know. I can't feel anything.
Count She is probably in shock.
Frau Lurker (*nodding*) Ja. There will be no pain—just *blood*.
Baron Shut up!
Countess (*wide-eyed*) Oh look! He's doing it again!
Baroness (*desperately*) *No.*

The knife plunges again and the Baroness gives another scream. There is the same reaction from the others. The Mummy lifts the knife once more

Ygor (*jumping up and down*) Encore!
Baroness (*fiercely*) Ygor!
Ygor (*abashed*) Sorry, Mistress. (*He bites his knuckles and hides behind Frau Lurker*)
Baroness (*petulantly*) Will someone get me *off* here? Aaah!

The knife plunges a third time. The Mummy extracts it, then hands it to the Baron. The music ends

Isabel (*sounding disappointed*) Is that it?
Baron I think so. Unless he's going to do something with rabbits.
Mummy (*shaking its head*) Uh-uh.

It performs a grotesque bow and everyone apart from the Baroness applauds. The Lights return to normal as she rises to her feet

Baron How do you feel?
Baroness Fragile—but otherwise fine. (*To the Mummy*) If all you were chasing was an assistant, why didn't you say so? I'd have put on a tu-tu.
Mummy (*shrugging and spreading its hands*) M-u-u-h.
Baroness Well, I suppose it's too late now.
Count (*gazing round*) Where is Mr Talbot?

Talbot enters L

Talbot Here. (*He now looks completely normal*) What the hell's been happenin'?
Countess A short parlour entertainment.

Talbot (*rubbing his head irritably*) Oh yeah?

Isabel You shoulda seen it. It was ace!

Talbot (*grimly*) Well the lump on my head ain't. When I get my paws on the bastard who——! (*Sharply*) Where *is* he?

There is a loud thumping from inside the mummy case

Baroness (*pointing*) In there.

The Count unlocks the lid and a dazed Dr Jekyll emerges, now his normal self

Jekyll (*with feeling*) 'Pon ma soul, that was a most *rum* proceedin'. Most rum indeed. Thought I was locked in a torture device—what with all those green things nibblin' me.

Baroness } (*together*) *Green* things?
Baron

Jekyll Ay! (*Pointing*) Take a look.

Everyone does so. The Baroness gives a shriek of delight and pulls Cabbage out of the case, hugging it

Baroness It's Cabbage!

Baron (*staring into the case*) And *babies*. (*Reaching down, he extracts a handful of small green objects*) By all that's broccoli—Cabbage has had sprouts!

Ygor (*to Frau Lurker, puzzled*) I thought you said——

Frau Lurker (*sharply*) I did not! My cuisine does not involve *rodents*.

Ygor (*wryly*) Not even your special?

Frau Lurker (*quickly*) Shut up!

Count (*to Jekyll*) What has become of Mr Hyde?

Jekyll He's gone, man. Gone for good.

Baron Are you sure?

Jekyll Positive. His last cry to me, as I was surfacin' into consciousness, was that he was bein' squeezed into oblivion. (*He rubs his throat*) Into the dark void from whence he came.

Ygor (*ecstatic*) Yippee!

Jekyll (*nodding*) Indeed, laddie—indeed. (*At large*) What's been brewin' with the rest o' ye? Did the potion work?

Count So that's what it was.

Countess I wondered what could have caused such strange——

Talbot *I'll* say!

Countess (*smiling*)—yet amusing effects. Was it you who laced our drinks, Doctor?

Jekyll No, no—it was Hyde bein' devilish as usual. But tell me—none o' ye are experiencin' any unpleasant reactions at all?

All (*with certainty*) No.

Jekyll (*rubbing his hands*) Splendid! Splendid! In that case, ye've nothin' more to fear . . .

Isabel How come?

Jekyll (*pointedly*) Ye're now normal. *All* of ye.

As they stare at each other in wonder the sound of Elgar's "Nimrod" is heard and builds throughout the next speech

Ye need no longer fear the scourges o' society for your faults. Ye may walk peacefully through the streets o' civilization with your heads held high—immune from unnatural despair, despicable appetites or malevolent tendencies. No deformity o' body or character shall beset ye. The moon shall hold no more terror—the sun will be your friend. An' when *sleep* comes, at the end of a perfect day, it will be the untroubled sleep o' the *righteous*!

The music reaches a crescendo and then the door R *bursts open to admit a creature from our worst nightmare (on Elm Street?)*

Creature (*malevolently*) *Wanna bet?*

As everyone on stage reacts:

IT'S SUPPERTIME!

All (*terrified*) Aaaah!

They flee in all directions as the Creature laughs maniacally and—

—the CURTAIN *falls*

FURNITURE AND PROPERTY LIST

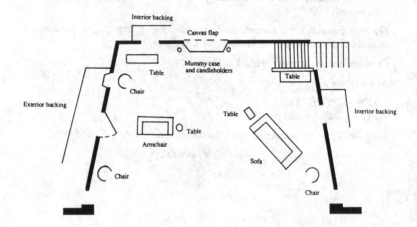

ACT I

On stage: Large mummy case with hinged or removable lid, painted with Egyptian hieroglyphics *Over it:* a dark velvet cloth (See *Special Effects* for further details about this and other items)
A very old sofa. *On it:* cushions. *Behind it:* hairy gloves, tail-bulge
A very old armchair. *Behind it:* wolf's tail
Three ornate high-backed chairs
Carved oak table (up R) *On it:* silver candelabra
Carved oak table (up L) *On it:* old-fashioned decanters and glasses
Two small tables
Two large candleholders
On walls: grim coats of arms, fearsome weapons (including a trick knife), tattered heraldic banners
Stone floor
Cobwebs and dust

Off stage: Wicker cat-box containing "Cabbage" **(Baroness)**
Huge spider on web **(Stage Management)**
Suitcase **(Frau Lurker)**
Suitcase **(Ygor)**

Spider **(Stage Management)**
Small suitcase **(Isabel)**
Rucksack **(Talbot)**
Spider **(Stage Management)**
"Cabbage" **(Baroness)**
Walking-stick, doctor's bag **(Jekyll)**

Personal: **Countess:** volume of poetry
Baron: notebook, pen, pocket watch, letter, tissue
Baroness: jewellery (required throughout)
Isabel: automatic flash camera (practical)
Count: pocket watch

ACT II

SCENE 1

Set: Mummy and scroll in mummy case

Off stage: Dead rat **(Frau Lurker)**
Walking-stick, doctor's bag containing flask of colourless liquid **(Jekyll)**
Tray with nine cocktail goblets **(Groat)**
Two dishes containing pretzels and marshmallows **(Ethel)**

Personal: **Baron:** small canister
Frau Lurker: tissue

SCENE 2

Off stage: Spider **(Stage Management)**
Weapons **(Frau Lurker** and **Ygor)**
Sword **(Talbot)**
Blank-firing revolver **(Baron)**

SCENE 3

Set: Wolf's tail behind sofa cushion
Cabbage and sprouts in mummy case

Off stage: Large book **(Baron)**
Whip **(Frau Lurker)**

Personal: **Baron:** small canister
Talbot: stage blood

LIGHTING PLOT

Property fittings required: candlelights

Interior. The hall of an ancient castle. The same scene throughout

ACT I   Late evening

To open: Gloomy candlelight with menacing shadows

Cue 1	**Baroness:** "Honestly, Victor, you should learn braille." *Lightning flickers*	(Page 16)
Cue 2	**Talbot:** "What are you sayin'?" *A flash of lightning*	(Page 16)
Cue 3	**Baron:** "Chas and Di couldn't possibly live here." *A flash of lightning*	(Page 16)
Cue 4	Following thunder-clap *An eerie light floods the stairs briefly*	(Page 17)
Cue 5	**Count:** "Good-evening, everyone." *A vivid flash of lightning*	(Page 17)
Cue 6	**Count:** "I am referring to *Walpurgisnacht*." *A flash of lightning*	(Page 19)
Cue 7	**Baron:** "I hate mysteries!" *An eerie light floods the stairs briefly*	(Page 24)
Cue 8	**Countess:** "I leave *that* to the rats." *Lightning flickers*	(Page 26)
Cue 9	As the **Countess** raises her arms in fury *Lightning flickers*	(Page 26)
Cue 10	**Countess:** ". . . brewing a noxious bean curd." *Lightning flickers*	(Page 26)
Cue 11	**Baron:** ". . . explore unknown powers—" *A flash of lightning*	(Page 27)
Cue 12	**Baron** and **Countess:** "Oh my God!" *Slow fade to black-out*	(Page 28)

ACT II, Scene 1.   Late evening

To open: As ACT I

Cue 13	**Jekyll:** "As if somethin' were *stirrin'*." *An eerie light floods the mummy case*	(Page 40)
Cue 14	As **All** race for the doors *Fade to black-out*	(Page 41)

ACT II, SCENE 2.

To open: As Scene 1

Cue 15	As the **Mummy** reaches for the **Count** and **Countess** *Crazy light effects begin*	(Page 41)
Cue 16	After the **Count** has chased the **Baroness** upstairs *The lights return to normal briefly*	(Page 41)
Cue 17	As the **Mummy** reaches out for **Isabel** *Crazy lights effects begin again*	(Page 42)
Cue 18	The **Count** shrugs and strides after the **Baron** *The lights fade to black-out*	(Page 42)

ACT II, SCENE 3.

To open: As Scene 1

Cue 19	**Baron:** "The fool's flipped." *An eerie light floods the stairs briefly*	(Page 46)
Cue 20	As **Isabel** is embraced by the **Count** *A flash of lightning*	(Page 51)
Cue 21	As the **Mummy** raises the knife over the **Baroness** *The lights focus on the sofa*	(Page 58)
Cue 22	As the **Baroness** rises from the sofa *The lights return to normal*	(Page 59)

EFFECTS PLOT

ACT I

Cue 18   **Baron:** "A Cyrillic C entwined with a D."   (Page 16)
           Thunder, growing closer

Cue 19   **Isabel:** ". . . don't own *this* place, surely?"   (Page 16)
           A louder roll of thunder

Cue 20   **Isabel:** "Who else signs himself *C.D.*?"   (Page 17)
           A loud thunder-clap

Cue 21   **All:** "Aaaah!"   (Page 17)
           A terrific thunder-clap

Cue 22   **Count:** ". . . not include sandwiches or crisps."   (Page 19)
           A hideous howl off

Cue 23   **Count:** "The Night of Terror!"   (Page 19)
           A roll of thunder

Cue 24   **Count:** "And things that go 'Yum!' in the night.   (Page 19)
           A hideous howl off

Cue 25   **Count:** ". . . battle the forces of evil."   (Page 20)
           Fading thunder

Cue 26   **Count:** "Solid as a rock."   (Page 23)
           Wolf howls off

Cue 27   **Count:** ". . . I have an appointment to keep."   (Page 24)
           The wolf howls cease

Cue 28   As the **Count** exits   (Page 24)
           Thunder rolls distantly

Cue 29   **Baron:** "I hate mysteries!"   (Page 24)
           Haunting music is heard briefly

Cue 30   **Countess:** ". . . seen to be believed."   (Page 25)
           An unearthly cry is heard off

Cue 31   **Countess:** ". . . to a pathetic old ruin."   (Page 25)
           More thunder is heard

Cue 32   **Countess:** ". . . in the catacombs below."   (Page 26)
           A louder roll of thunder

Cue 33   **Countess:** "Vampires detest vegetarianism."   (Page 26)
           Another roll of thunder

Cue 34   **Countess:** ". . . before the fumes reached them."   (Page 26)
           A hideous howl off

Cue 35   **Countess:** ". . . reading each other's feet."   (Page 27)
           Thunder again and a gale begins to blow

Cue 36   **Baron:** ". . . deepest mysteries of creation!"   (Page 27)
           A terrific thunder-clap followed by fierce gale and rain effects

Cue 37   As **Jekyll** pounds on the door   (Page 27)
           The gale fades slightly

Cue 38   As the door begins to open   (Page 28)
           Snarling and snapping sounds are heard off

Cue 39   As **Jekyll** laughs maniacally   (Page 28)
           The snarling and snapping ceases, but the gale and rain
           continue moderately

Cue 40   As **Jekyll** swings his stick, laughing madly   (Page 28)
           Sinister music begins

ACT II

Cue 41   Before the Curtain rises   (Page 29)
           Sinister music linked to howls, shrieks and roars

Cue 42   As the **Baron** slams the door   (Page 29)
           The howls cease and a roll of thunder is heard

Cue 43   As **Frau Lurker** throws back lid of mummy case   (Page 38)
           Cloud of fumes from inside

Cue 44   As the **Count** stands over **Jekyll** menacingly   (Page 39)
           Roll of thunder

Cue 45   After **Jekyll** throws contents of goblet into **Mummy**'s face   (Page 39)
           New clouds of fumes billow from case

Cue 46   **Jekyll:** "As if somethin' were *stirrin'*."   (Page 40)
           Eerie Egyptian music begins and continues to end of scene

Cue 47   As the Lights come up on Scene 2   (Page 41)
           A wolf howl is heard

Cue 48   As the **Mummy** chases the **Count** and **Countess** off   (Page 41)
           Atmospheric "chase" music begins

Cue 49   After the **Count** has chased the **Baroness** off   (Page 41)
           There is a pause in the music

Cue 50   As the **Mummy** chases **Isabel** off   (Page 42)
           The music begins again and continues to the end of the scene

Cue 51   As the Lights come up on Scene 3   (Page 42)
           Snarling and snapping sounds are heard off until **Jekyll** *enters*
           and slams the door

Cue 52   As the **Mummy** chases **Jekyll** off   (Page 44)
           A roll of thunder

Cue 53   **Baron:** ". . . life in a Cairo pet-shop."   (Page 45)
           Howls and cries are heard off

Cue 54   As the door opens   (Page 45)
           The howls get louder

Cue 55   After the **Baron** throws the canister off   (Page 46)
           A small explosion is heard. The howls cease

Cue 56   **Baron:** "What in blazes is *going on* here?"   (Page 47)
           A bell tolls in an eerie wind

Cue 57 As **Frau Lurker** chases **Ygor** off (Page 48)
The bell and wind effect ceases

Cue 58 **Countess:** ". . . in the morning. If not *two*." (Page 48)
A romantic tune begins

Cue 59 **Baron:** ". . . *substantial* on this occasion." (Page 49)
The tune ends

Cue 60 As the **Count** moves towards the **Countess** (Page 49)
A roll of thunder

Cue 61 **Count:** "It does indeed." (Page 50)
Dance music begins

Cue 62 As the **Countess** exits (Page 51)
The music ends

Cue 63 Immediately following the lightning flash (Page 51)
A roll of thunder

Cue 64 As the **Count** exits (Page 52)
A fading roll of thunder

Cue 65 **Ygor** (*terrified*): "Yes—yes! *Help*!" (Page 55)
Wolf howl, off

Cue 66 **Talbot:** "Mates of mine have come callin!" (Page 56)
Wolf howl, off

Cue 67 **Talbot:** "Those sure felt like—*growin'* pains." (Page 56)
Wolf howl, off

Cue 68 As the **Mummy** enters (Page 57)
Sinister music

Cue 69 As the **Mummy** lets **Hyde** slide to the floor (Page 58)
The music ends

Cue 70 As the **Mummy** raises the knife over the **Baroness** (Page 58)
Lively Egyptian music begins

Cue 71 As the **Mummy** hands the knife to the **Baron** (Page 59)
The music ends

Cue 73 **Jekyll:** "Ye're now normal. *All* of ye." (Page 60)
Elgar's "Nimrod" begins

Cue 74 **Jekyll:** ". . . untroubled sleep o' the righteous!" (Page 61)
The music reaches a crescendo then ceases

Cue 75 As the **Creature** laughs maniacally (Page 61)
Appropriate sinister music for Curtain

NB: For convenience I have not listed all the pounding on the door, screams or yells, as these can be managed by the members of the cast or crew.

COSTUME SUGGESTIONS

Baron. Edwardian travelling clothes. Top hat. Evening wear. Smoking jacket.

Baroness. Edwardian travelling clothes. Gloves. Evening dress. Diamond necklace, ear-rings and bracelets. Négligé.

Ygor. Ill-fitting butler's outfit. Large hump. Night-shirt.

Frau Lurker. Black coat over Victorian housekeeper's dress. Hat. Gloves. Floor-length nightie. Black leather outfit.

Talbot. Leather jacket, macho shirt, jeans and trainers. Tuxedo, dress shirt etc. White T-shirt, shorts and socks—i.e. a typical PE strip.

Isabel. Shapeless coat over garish flapper's outfit. Hat. Gloves. Bangles and beads. Equally loud evening dress and clashing jewellery. Short night-dress.

Count. Black 18th century costume. Cloak. Formal evening wear.

Countess. Black 18th century gown. Veil and gloves. Stunning evening dress and jewellery. (Neither she nor the Count need to wear night attire.)

Jekyll. Greatcoat over Victorian evening wear. Top hat. Gloves.

Groat. A dusty/mouldy footman's outfit.

Ethel. A trailing white or grey dress—early 13th century.

Ka-Seet. A close-fitting outfit which appears to be mummy wrappings because of shreds and tatters here and there.

Spectre and **Creature.** See Character Descriptions on page viii.

SPECIAL EFFECTS

The mummy case. Constructed to an approximately authentic shape (curves may be difficult) and painted as described, it can be built into a door flat with the sides and front projecting on to the set and a loose canvas flap forming the back. This is ideal for two reasons; (1) so the Mummy doesn't have to spend too much time inside it, and (2) dry ice can be pumped into it from the back of the set to simulate fumes. Similarly this allows Cabbage and "sprouts" to be placed there at the end of Act II.

Cabbage. This is something half-guinea-pig, half vegetable. Any leafy variations are possible, but the main thing is it's *green*. The "sprouts" can be just that.

The spider. A huge, realistic Black Widow. It should descend on its web (operated from the wings via a pulley system) head downwards. The four back legs can be rigid, but the four at the front should move horribly.

Talbot. Before the play begins he should be given slightly pointed hairy ears which last until he emerges normal at the end of Act II.

Act I: The next wolfish elements are the hairy hands and tail-bulge which he acquires after Isabel has taken photographs of him. The hands can simply be hairy gloves; the tail-bulge is a sizeable stiff ball of fabric which he can push down the back of his jeans while he is crouching behind the sofa. Later in the action, when he bounds behind the armchair, he swaps this last item for a short bushy tail. It should be fairly rigid and constructed in such a way that it can be hooked over the waistband of his jeans without it slipping or falling off. All of these items have to be set in position before the Curtain rises.

Act II. For much of the act he looks relatively normal, apart from his ears, but during his pseudo-transformation in Scene 3, when he should convince the audience that he *is* becoming a wolf, he attaches a large tail to the back of his shorts. This should be of similar construction to the one above, but because it's larger the waistband of his shorts must be close-fitting to hold it in place. The parts of the tails which hook over can be concealed by his jacket and T-shirt respectively. At the end of the play, when he emerges from the doorway L, he should look completely normal.
NB: Body make-up should be used for Scene 3.

The Vampires. Use tooth whitener on the canines and tooth black on the lower half of their incisors to create fangs. Joke teeth are not successful.

Make-up. You should be as adventurous as possible, but try to avoid visual clichés—i.e. making the Count and Countess resemble Bela Lugosi or Morticia. The Mummy's face should resemble a dried-up prune and Groat's is as decayed as you can manage.

Dry ice. This is a must for the Mummy's resurrection, but it can also drift in through the castle door at appropriate moments.

Lighting. Generally eerie, but additional atmosphere can be created by lighting Frau Lurker with a green spot whenever she's predicting likely horrors. Also, as each character drinks the potion (preferably C), a flickering spot above them creates a wonderful image.

Martin Downing 1991.

MADE AND PRINTED IN GREAT BRITAIN BY
LATIMER TREND & COMPANY LTD PLYMOUTH
MADE IN ENGLAND